EXETER MEDIEVAL ENGLISH TEXTS AND STUDIES

General Editors: Marion Glasscoe and M.J. [ ] n

EXETER MEDIEVAL ENGLISH TEXTS AND STUDIES

A full list of titles in the Exeter Medieval English Texts and Studies series
is available from the University of Exeter Press, Reed Hall,
Streatham Drive, Exeter, Devon EX4 4QR, UK.

The Seafarer

Edited by
IDA GORDON

with a Bibliography compiled by
MARY CLAYTON

UNIVERSITY
of
EXETER
PRESS

First published in the Methuen Old English Library
and reissued in 1979 in the Old and Middle English Texts series
by Manchester University Press.

First published, with a new Bibliography by Mary Clayton,
in 1996 in the Exeter Medieval English Texts and Studies Series by

University of Exeter Press
Reed Hall, Streatham Drive
Exeter, Devon EX4 4QR
UK

British Library Cataloguing in Publication Data
A catalogue record for this book is available
from the British Library.

ISBN 0 85989 507 6

Printed in Great Britain
by BPC Wheatons Ltd

Contents

v

Contents

Preface

When my husband, Professor E. V. Gordon, died in 1938 he left an uncompleted draft of an edition of *The Wanderer* and *The Seafarer*, on which he had been working in collaboration with Professor J. R. R. Tolkien. And my first intention, with Professor Tolkien's approval, was to bring into final form that edition. But by the time I was free to begin the work there had been a revolution in the study of these poems. Articles had been published which threw new light on their themes and opened up new fields of investigation. And it soon became clear that the approach would have to be very different from that of the original draft, and that the treatment also would have to be much fuller, since many conflicting theories had been offered, which in themselves raised new problems of interpretation. To keep the edition to a size compatible with the plan of the series it was necessary therefore to confine it to one poem, and I chose *The Seafarer* for its more challenging theme. I have submitted the edition under my own name because it represents a view of the poem basically different from that of the original draft. Nevertheless the edition incorporates much of the original material, especially in the Notes. Without this initial help my task would have been much harder, and the edition would no doubt have contained more errors.

I wish to thank Professor Tolkien for some notes given to me with his usual generosity, and Mrs Joan Turville-Petre, who was kind enough to read an earlier draft of this edition, and whose valuable criticisms and suggestions helped to determine its present form, and Dr F. E. Harmer for helpful advice.

This edition of *The Seafarer* (the first separate edition) is based on the text as it appears in the facsimile edition of *The Exeter Book*. References throughout will indicate its indebtedness to previous editions and commentaries. An attempt has

PREFACE

been made to assess the various theories of interpretation, and
to relate the poem and its problems to the literary and intellectual background of the period.

The Victoria University, Manchester   I. L. GORDON
May, 1959

Abbreviations

AfdA	*Anzeiger für deutsches Altertum und deutsche Literatur*
Archiv	*Archiv für das Studium der neueren Sprachen und Literaturen*
Beiträge	*Beiträge zur Geschichte der deutschen Sprache und Literatur*
BT	J. Bosworth and T. N. Toller, *An Anglo-Saxon Dictionary*, 1882 (*Suppl.* 1921)
EDD	*English Dialect Dictionary*
E.E.T.S.	Early English Text Society
ESt	*Englische Studien*
JEGPh	*Journal of English and Germanic Philology*
MLN	*Modern Language Notes*
MLR	*Modern Language Review*
OE	Old English
ON	Old Norse
ONorth	Old Northumbrian
RES	*Review of English Studies*
ZfdA	*Zeitschrift für deutsches Altertum und deutsche Literatur*
ZfdPh	*Zeitschrift für deutsche Philologie*

Introduction

THE MANUSCRIPT

The unique text of *The Seafarer* is on folios 81ᵇ–83ᵃ of the
Exeter Book, presented to the Library of Exeter Cathedral by
Bishop Leofric not later than 1072, and still preserved there. A
facsimile of the manuscript was published in 1933, with a full
description of its history and handwriting, by R. W. Chambers,
M. Förster and R. Flower, and for detailed information the
reader is referred to their authoritative account.[1] It need only
be said here that Flower assigns the handwriting to the
period 970–90, and to the earlier decade rather than the
later, and considers it likely to have been written in the west
of Wessex. The pages containing *The Seafarer* are clear and
undamaged.

THEME AND STRUCTURE

The text of the poem has clearly suffered during transmission
to its present form. There are several scribal errors affecting
single letters or words; a half-line appears to be missing in line
16; alliteration is lacking in line 25; and in the last part of the
poem, from line 103, there are signs of mutilation and possibly
interpolation.[2] The poem has suffered still more, however, at
the hands of editors and commentators. The unusual difficulties its theme and structure present have proved a tempta-
tion to theorists who, all too often, have shown scant respect
for the poem as it stands. Thus some would end at line 102,
some would have us believe that the original consisted of the
seafaring part only, to line 64ᵃ, the rest being the work of a

---

[1] See also K. Sisam, *Studies in the History of Old English Literature*, chap. 6
'The Exeter Book', 97–108.
[2] See below, p. 11.

Christian reviser, and some have even distinguished originally independent poems in the seafaring part itself.[1]

Much Old English poetry is composite in the sense that it draws freely on a common poetic stock, and *The Seafarer* is no exception. But such use of inherited, or borrowed, matter is not sufficient ground for assuming that the poem is not a unity. And though there is an apparently abrupt change of thought at line 64, where the real seafaring theme ends and a not very obviously connected moralizing begins, the two parts are closely linked grammatically and metrically,[2] and the difference of style between them is no greater than the difference of subject matter warrants. There are, in fact, no reasons for denying integrity to the poem except the difficulty of tracing in it a connected theme. And in the more recent analyses various 'interpretations' of the seafaring theme have been offered which are directed mainly to that end. Though there is considerable diversity in these interpretations, each has added something and helped to show that the answer to its problems should be sought, not in dismembering the poem, but in a clearer understanding both of its theme and of the genre to which it belongs.

One difficulty which the poem seemed to present has, happily, been overcome by this better understanding which more recent study has reached. It was commonly thought at one time that the seafaring theme showed such inconsistent attitudes towards the sea that it must be intended to represent a dialogue between an old seafarer who recalls the hardships of his voyage and a young man eager to set sail. But W. W. Lawrence showed the weakness of this theory,[3] and it is now generally accepted that the seafaring theme represents the reflections of a man who knows from experience the dangers and

---

[1] For accounts of these various less recent views see W. W. Lawrence, '*The Wanderer and the Seafarer*', *JEGPh* iv. (1902) 460 ff; N. Kershaw, *Anglo-Saxon and Norse Poems* (1922) 16 f; and O. S. Anderson, '*The Seafarer*: an Interpretation', *K. Humanistiska Vetenskapssamfundets i Lund Årsberättelse* I (1937–8).

[2] I.e. the transition occurs within a sentence, and there is no break in the metre.

[3] *loc. cit.* 460–71. Attention is drawn to *Prose Edda* (pp. 51–52 in Jean Young's translation) where similar contradictory attitudes to the sea are expressed in verses by Njord, god of the sea, and his wife Skadi.

hardships of seafaring, and yet feels a longing to make a voyage across the ocean. What is not now generally accepted, however, is Lawrence's interpretation of the Seafarer's motive – that he is drawn by the call of the sea itself. For there is nothing in the text itself to support this interpretation. Until line 33[b] the Seafarer is reflecting on the miseries of his experiences of seafaring, contrasting his sufferings with the pleasures and comforts of life on land. And so the thoughts trouble [1] his heart now that he himself must venture on the deep (or towering) seas (33[b]–35). The use of *sylf* implies that, though he has had experience of seafaring, he has not himself before made such a journey across the ocean. And he now tells of the longing which urges him to make the journey to 'seek the land (or home) of aliens far hence' (36–8). And after this apparently parenthetic explanation of why he is about to venture on the ocean, he dwells on the difficulties and dangers of the journey: for there is no man on earth, however fortunate his circumstances, who does not have anxiety always on (or about) his sea-voyage as to what the Lord may purpose for him (39–43). His thought is not on the pleasures of the world, but only on the rolling of the waves; for he who ventures on the sea has always a troubled mind [2] (44–7). The signs of spring urge to his journey one who is minded to travel far over the ocean (48–52). The sad voice of the cuckoo, boding bitter sorrow to the heart, also urges (53–55[a]). And though he still reflects on the sufferings of exile which those blessed with comfort do not know (55[b]–57), his spirit escapes from the confines of his breast to travel far over the ocean, and returns to him again eager and hungering (58–62[a]). The lone-flier [3] calls, inciting him irresistibly over the sea, be-

---

[1] This is the usual figurative meaning of *cnyssan*, but the basic meaning is 'beat against', and the sentence may mean that his thoughts are pressing him to venture on the ocean. That interpretation makes the transition of thought more abrupt, but is not in itself out of keeping with what follows in the poem, and the awkwardness of *For þon* could be explained away by taking it as correlative with *for þon* in line 39 (the first *For þon* need not then be translated in modern idiom).

[2] For a discussion of the meaning of *longunge* see below, p. 7.

[3] See note to l. 62[b].

cause 'the joys of the Lord' (i.e. heavenly life) are warmer (more living) to him than 'this dead, transitory life on land' (62^b–66^a).

The abruptness with which this explicit Christian motive for the Seafarer's journey is introduced need no longer cast doubt on its genuineness as an integral part of the theme. For as we shall see later, there have been implicit verbal indications from line 33^b onwards that the Seafarer's journey has a Christian significance, and lines 64^b–66^a, which imply that the journey is for the purpose of gaining the bliss of Heaven, must be accepted as the exposition of that Christian significance, and the seafaring theme must be considered more fully in relation to them.

But different views have been taken of the seafaring theme in relation to these lines. G. Ehrismann,[1] L. L. Schücking,[2] O. S. Anderson [3] and G. V. Smithers [4] have taken the lines in a symbolic sense and interpreted the whole seafaring theme as an allegory. They see in the picture of the hardships of seafaring in the early part of the poem an allegorical representation of the afflictions of life, but whereas Ehrismann sees in the Seafarer's longing to make a voyage across the sea the monastic ideal of asceticism as opposed to the materialistic view of life represented by those who live on land, Anderson, following Schücking, believes that voyage to be, 'not only the life of the pious on earth, but also life as the road to eternity, and in this sense also death'.[5] G. V. Smithers takes a similar view, but he arrives at it by specific reference to patristic and vernacular writings where metaphors of the 'wanderer' or *peregrinus* (over the sea) symbolize man as an exile from Paradise, and the process of these wanderings symbolizes his *peregrinatio* on earth (with reference to his ancestral home in Heaven). Dr Dorothy White-

[1] 'Religionsgeschichtliche Beiträge zum germanischen Frühchristentum', *Beiträge* xxxv (1909). 213–18.

[2] *ESt* li (1917). 105–9.

[3] *op. cit.* (see above, p. 2, note 1), 10 ff.

[4] 'The Meaning of *The Seafarer* and *The Wanderer*', *Medium Ævum* xxvi. no. 3 (1957). 137–53.

[5] *op. cit.* 12–34.

lock, on the other hand, observing that there is no indication in the text that the poem was intended to be an allegory, takes lines 62^b–66^a in a literal sense to imply that the Seafarer is intended to suggest a 'real' *peregrinus* or pilgrim-hermit, who wishes to earn the bliss of Heaven by seeking in the loneliness and rigours of exile a less worldly life.[1] She shows by ample historical evidence that such a figure would be familiar enough to an Anglo-Saxon audience. Mr. E. G. Stanley regards the poem as 'neither realism nor allegory', but 'an imagined situation, invented to give force to the doctrine which forms the end of the poem and is its purpose'. He contends that 'exile combines within its natural situation all the misery which OE poetry expressed by the anguish of solitude, darkness, cold. The nature of OE poetry is such that there is no means of separating fact from figure. Factually or figuratively, it is miseries such as these that a man must flee to, if he sees no lasting hope in this dead life of worldly joys.'[2]

The strongest argument for an allegorical interpretation is the evidence cited by Mr Smithers to show that 'exile' or 'sojourn as an alien' was applied in ecclesiastical tradition to Adam and his descendants, and that the concept applied to good Christians only, who are *peregrini* or 'aliens' in this world because they belong to the city of God, in contrast to those who are 'citizens' of this world. As Mr Smithers remarks: 'The currency of the contrast, by Anglo-Saxon times, owed a great deal to St Augustine's elaboration of it in *De Civitate Dei*, and of the idea that there are two *civitates*, of men who live *secundum Deum* and *secundum hominem* respectively.'[3] The Seafarer represents one who lives *secundum Deum* and longs to make the journey to seek *elþeodigra eard*, which (metaphorically) is the (heavenly) home of those who are 'aliens' in this world;[4]

---

[1] 'The Interpretation of *The Seafarer*', in *Early Cultures of North-West Europe, H. M. Chadwick Memorial Studies* (1950). 261–72.

[2] 'Old English Poetic Diction and the Interpretation of *The Wanderer, The Seafarer* and *The Penitent's Prayer*', *Anglia* lxxiii (1955). 453–4.

[3] *loc. cit.* 147.

[4] *ibid.* 151.

while 'those whose lot is cast most happily on land' are *cives* of this world who find their happiness here on earth.

Perhaps the strongest argument against an allegorical interpretation of *The Seafarer* is that allegory is not explicit in the poem, and that the tone of lament and the general poetic pattern suggests elegy rather than allegory, especially in an age when the personal elegiac lament was a popular genre. Yet even those who are not inclined to see in the seafaring theme a purely allegorical device may feel that there are peculiarities in its presentation which prevent them from accepting it simply as the reflections of a *peregrinus*, real or imagined. For the impression given by the Seafarer's reflections does not suggest a spiritual attitude, as, for instance, do the Irish hermit poems. Instead, it is the sea-journey itself, as a physical experience, that dominates the theme. Even when the Christian implications of the journey come nearest to the surface, as, for instance, in lines 44-5 (one who goes to sea has no thought for worldly pleasures), it is always with reference to the seafaring image ('nor for anything else except the rolling of the waves'). Mr Stanley would attribute this to the nature of Old English poetic diction, which chose to express the misery inherent in the situation of exile in such terms. But though this explanation may help to account to some extent for the form in which the theme is cast, it is not enough to answer all the problems. One of the main aims of early Christian exiles was to attain the peacefulness of the hermit's life, free from disturbing emotion and stress, whereas the Seafarer seems to be drawn by the very troubles and dangers involved in the journey: the cuckoo's voice, boding bitter sorrow, urges him to go, and it is the life on land he is renouncing that is free from troubles.

The reason why the emphasis has been on the sea-journey itself is revealed in lines 64^b–66^a, when the motive for the journey is made explicit. For at this point the 'life on land' becomes 'this dead, transitory life' (the worldly life of mortal man) which is 'dead' because it is less warm and living to him than 'the joys of the Lord'. In the light of this transformation the sea-journey becomes not only the personal act of one who prefers the difficulties and dangers of the sea to the comforts and pleasures of life on land, but also an act symbolic of the renunciation of worldly life generally and the ready acceptance of the struggles and sufferings involved in the quest for eternal bliss. And it is as a symbolic act that the Seafarer's journey serves as a bridge to the wider, more universal theme of the second half of the poem, which is a homily on the transitory nature of earthly prosperity and happiness and the importance of preparing for the life hereafter.

If we look more closely at the poem we see that the symbolism which comes to the surface in lines $64^b–66^a$ is inherent earlier in ambiguous forms of expression, where behind the literal meaning there is a suggestion of a deeper, more universal significance. Thus lines 39–43, which refer on a literal level to the hazards of sea-voyaging, are an adaptation of the familiar homiletic theme that there is no man on earth, however fortunate his circumstances, who does not have to face death, and the wording of line 43 also echoes homiletic warnings of the Doom to come (see note). Similarly in line 47, *ac a hafað longunge se þe on lagu fundað*, while *longunge* here in its literal application appears to denote the anxiety that a seafarer must feel, it carries also a connotation of the yearning that comes from unsatisfied desire,[1] and again the general nature of the statement suggests that the situation of a seafarer is intended to symbolize the situation of all who yearn for something beyond 'this dead and transitory life'. And in line 50, *modes fusne* 'eager of heart', which applies literally to a readiness to face the physical dangers and discomforts of a seajourney, has also a Christian connotation of spiritual readiness to face death,[2] and once more the general nature of the statement helps to suggest a universal application. It is a feature of the poet's method to play thus on the meaning of terms which had both secular and Christian associations,[3] and there are too many of these ambiguous passages for them to be accidental.

---

[1] See D. Whitelock, *loc. cit.* 265, note 1.

[2] Cf. the opening line of the Epilogue to *Elene*: *þus ic frod ond fus* . . .

[3] See below, p. 26 f.

They illustrate the typical medieval tendency to see a situation simultaneously under different aspects, each independent and existing on its own level, but at the same time forming part of a transcendent whole.

All this, however, does not make the seafaring theme into an allegory. Symbolism can suggest or imply ideas of a higher order or a more universal significance without being confined within a determinate allegorical system, and the question whether a work is allegorical or not must depend on the literary intention as it appears in the form in which the work is cast. The obstinate wife of Noah, when she refuses to go into the Ark because she will not believe God's warning of the Flood, is both an example of individual lack of faith on a particular occasion and also a symbol of all who will not believe in the Wrath to come and will not accept in time the means of salvation offered to them. But this is not allegory, because the primary literary intention is the representation of the actual situation. In *The Seafarer* the literal situation is not an actual one in the same factual sense, but it is actual in the sense that it is, in its own right, in the forefront of the poetic effect and intention. We have evidence that the theme of exile was a favourite theme of lyric-elegy as a situation in which physical and emotional experiences could be explored for their own sake,[1] and in *The Seafarer* this lyric-elegiac theme has been developed and exploited for a symbolic purpose, to illustrate the *peregrinatio* of good Christians towards their heavenly home. But it does not become thereby merely a convenient expression for the ecclesiastical metaphor. It retains its lyric-elegiac character, which conveys or illuminates on a physical and emotional level the actual experience of what is symbolized. The method is that of the medieval symbolic religious lyric rather than allegory.

An example of the dangers involved in an allegorical interpretation of the poem, which would see in the seafaring theme in its entirety something other than itself, is provided by Mr Smithers' attempt to prove that the Seafarer's journey is an

[1] See below, p. 15 ff.

allegory of death. His evidence to show that the metaphor of man as an 'alien' or 'exile' in this world lies behind the phrase *elþeodigra eard gesece* of line 38 certainly provides convincing corroboration of what is implied in lines 64^b–66^a, namely that the Seafarer's longing to cross the ocean is a longing to seek his heavenly home, the home of those who are 'aliens' in this world. But it does not follow that the journey signifies death itself. *Elþeodig*, as Mr Smithers demonstrates, translates Latin *peregrinus*, used metaphorically. But *peregrinus* in the same metaphorical sense is also used of a cloistered monk (who lives in this world as a 'pilgrim' to God). The verb *peregrinari* similarly is used metaphorically to mean 'withdraw to a monastery', 'lead the life of a cloistered monk', just as the Irish monks speak of 'seeking the place of their salvation'.[1] Thus when the Seafarer longs to make a journey to seek *elþeodigra eard*, his journey need not signify death itself. Any act of positive renunciation of the world and its pleasures becomes a *peregrinatio* to the home of *peregrini* (in heaven).

Mr Smithers attempts to substantiate his view, that the Seafarer's journey signifies death, by a new interpretation of lines 58–64^a, which he takes to be a description of 'the launching of the soul (*hyge*) on the *wælweg*' ('the road taken by the dead' or 'the road to the abode of the dead')'.[2] But the evidence for *wælweg* is unconvincing (see note to line 63), and he does not explain why the launched soul should return again eager and hungering, or why it should cry out (*gielleð*). A more probable interpretation is that the Seafarer's spirit momentarily leaves its bodily prison (*hreþerlocan*) and ranges far over the path of ocean that the Seafarer longs to take in reality, and returns to him again eager and hungering to start the journey; and (as he returns to consciousness of his surroundings) he hears the lone-flying cuckoo calling (as it called to him immediately before this imaginative or visionary experience), inciting him to the journey – this time irresistibly, because 'the joys of the Lord' (when the spirit will have escaped for ever from the confines of

[1] See Mrs N. K. Chadwick, *Poetry and Letters in Early Christian Gaul*, 186.
[2] *loc. cit.* 137 ff and 151 f.

9

the flesh) are now more real and living to him than 'this dead, transitory life on land'. Here the ranging aspiration and fierce determination of lines 58–63 are explained: the vain and fleeting pleasures and comforts of this world ('life on land') are to be left behind, and the suffering exacted by God from his followers (the *sorge* of the sea-journey) is to be undertaken with eagerness in the quest for eternity. The Seafarer does not choose death; he responds with eager longing to the challenge of that suffering.

Mr Smithers claims that the launching of the soul on the *wælweg* is necessary to provide the transition between the seafaring theme and the universal topics of the second half of the poem.[1] But the transition is provided explicitly in the poem itself when 'life on land' is equated with 'this dead, transitory life'. Up to this point the method of presentation has been similar to that which we find in some of the later medieval lyrics (e.g. *Maiden in the Mor Lay*), where the theme is deliberately enigmatic so that the reader is forced to seek out an underlying significance. Lines 64b–66a bring that underlying significance to the surface, and make the Seafarer's journey into an *exemplum* in physical terms of the spiritual lesson that is expounded in the remaining part of the poem: that the quest for eternity is more vital to man than the material benefits of this world. But the main intention of the seafaring theme is not the conveying of this abstract moral idea in concrete terms. The poetic genre to which the poem belongs is one in which the meaning of human situations is developed and exploited in the form of reflective dramatic monologue, and the most plausible explanation of the form and theme of *The Seafarer* is that it is an imaginative evocation of physical and emotional experiences that are used to illuminate a symbolic spiritual truth.

At line 66b the poem leaves the theme of seafaring and turns wholly to its homiletic theme. Earthly prosperity will not last for ever; though it remains a matter of uncertainty until his final hour how death will come to a man, come it will to every

[1] *loc. cit.* 151–2.

one (66^b–71). And so the best memorial a man can leave behind him is the posthumous glory which he may win by his
Christian conduct here on earth, which will gain him also the
glory of eternal happiness (72–80^a). And as a contrast to this
eternal glory we are reminded of the brief nature of earthly
power and glory (80^b–90), and of the dissolution and decay
that come with old age and death (91–6), and how gold,
whether it be lavished by a brother at his brother's grave or
hoarded while he lived here on earth, cannot help the soul of
the sinful man in face of the awful power of God (97–102).

Some editors would end the poem here, assuming that what
follows, which is mainly gnomic statement and Christian admonition of a derivative and conventional kind, is a later ad-
dition. And the fact that line 102 ends at the bottom of a folio
might be held to support this view. But it is less abrupt, as well
as more fitting to a homiletic theme, that the poem should end
with some direct Christian admonition and prayer, as does
The Wanderer, which is otherwise very similar to *The Seafarer* in
construction. Exactly what portion or portions of what remains
should be regarded as original is a more difficult question. The
lack of coherence and evidence of textual corruption after line
108 make it tempting to assume that the poem should end
there. Yet lines 113–115^a, which are among the most corrupt,
bear a resemblance in verbal pattern to lines 97–102, and if we
emend MS *hine* of line 113 to *ne* they repeat in a different form
one of the ideas expressed in the earlier passage, the futility of
hoping to help one's near ones on the Day of Judgement:
'Though he may not wish the friend he has made to burn in
the fire [of Hell], Doom is more powerful, God mightier than
any man's conception.' The relevance of these lines to what
goes immediately before them, as they stand, is not clear, and
it is possible that they have been misplaced by the insertion of
material that did not belong to the original poem. That there
has been some interpolation, and possibly re-arrangement, may
perhaps be indicated by the fact that the gnomic statements of
lines 109–12 are not an essential part of the particular stylized
homiletic pattern which the second half of *The Seafarer* is

clearly following.[1] Nor are lines 107–8, although, as advocating the virtue of humility, they are relevant to a homiletic theme in a general way. Otherwise all the ideas expressed in this last passage, from line 102, are relevant to the central theme. The world will be transformed [in the Final Hour] (103–5); foolish is he who does not fear his Lord, death will come upon him unprepared (106); and the final exhortation: 'Let us think where we have our home and let us strive to come thither . . .', conventional though it is, makes a fitting concluding summary of the whole homiletic theme.

GENESIS OF THE POEM: ANALOGUES AND INFLUENCES

The genesis of *The Seafarer* presents two separate and very different problems. The second part of the poem, from line 66[b], follows a familiar homiletic pattern which must have been known to the poet in an already well-defined form, and the difficulty here is to trace the immediate source. There is no evidence of any such specific source for the first, or seafaring, part, and its genesis presents a more complex problem, which has been approached from various angles. Thus Dr Whitelock puts the seafaring theme historically within the framework of Anglo-Saxon ideals of Christian renunciation and austerity; and Mr Stanley relates it further to the practices of Old English poetic diction. Mr Smithers rejects these explanations of its origins: he claims (with justice) that for a poem written 'in an age which exalted literary authority, and in which poetic themes and even forms are almost bound to be for this reason inherited ones',[2] a more specific explanation is needed. But his specific explanation, in the form of metaphors from ecclesiastical writings in which the 'exile' symbolizes man as an exile from Paradise, or the sea symbolizes human life on earth, only goes part way to explaining the origins of the seafaring theme. It is form as well as subject matter that is usually inherited in this early poetry, and Mr Smithers' evidence does not provide literary authority for the distinctive poetic form

---

[1] See below, p. 23 ff.   [2] *loc. cit.* 145.

the theme takes. For surely he pursues his case too far, at the expense of other aspects of the problem, when he quotes two examples where the notion of *erumna* 'trouble, hardship, misery' is used with reference to Adam's expulsion from Paradise, and adds: 'it (*erumna*) does more to explain the emphasis on hardship and sorrow in *The Seafarer* and *The Wanderer* than any reference to elegiac lament in such poems as *The Wife's Lament* and *Deor*'.[1]

We should not belittle the importance of these other poems in Old English where hardship and sorrow in association with the theme of exile form the subject of personal lyrical laments. It is because *The Wife's Lament* presents a similar poetic pattern, and even at times close parallels of thought and expression [2] that it is proper to consider it in relation to the first parts of *The Seafarer* and *The Wanderer*. All three are laments in which the speaker is an exile or wanderer, contrasting his (or her) lot with some happier state; in all three the feelings of the speaker evoke references to external natural surroundings and phenomena; and in all three the elegiac reflections lead to sententious admonition and gnomic statement. There is even in *The Wife's Lament* that same detachment from definite associations of name, time and place that Mr Smithers claims as support for his allegory theory in *The Seafarer* and *The Wanderer*.[3] If we are to seek literary authority for the theme of exile, hardship and misery in *The Seafarer* and *The Wanderer* we must not be content to find it only in metaphors expressed briefly in patristic writings; we must look also to the elegiac genre itself.

A full survey of that genre is impossible here, but some significant facts may be noted. There are two types of elegiac lament in Old English poetry: besides the type with which we are concerned, which we may call lyric-elegy, there is the more conventional plaint, in which the poet, usually in old age, looks back on his life, lamenting the joys of his youth and the

---

[1] *loc. cit.* 146.

[2] E.g. *Seaf.* 1–4: *Wife's Lament* 1–3; *Seaf.* 6: *Wife's Lament* 32^b, 41^b (*mec bigeat* used in an unusual sense); *Seaf.* 23: *Wife's Lament* 48: *Wand.* 76–7, 101.

[3] *ibid.* 149.

death of friends and kin, invokes the mercy of God and looks to the bliss of Heaven. Typical of such plaints are Cynewulf's Epilogues and the Author's Prayer at the end of *The Dream of the Rood*. The origins of such plaints are easy to trace in early Christian Latin poetry, where we find a similar preoccupation with the themes of old age, death and decay and the brevity of earthly happiness, expressed sometimes in the form of admonitory poems, such as Columbanus' *Ad Hunaldum Epistola* and *Ad Fedolium Epistola*,[1] sometimes in reflective, homiletic poems, such as Columbanus' *De Vanitate et Miseria Vitae Mortalis* [2] or the *De Brevitate hujus Vitae* of Eugenius of Toledo,[3] and sometimes in a form very similar to that of the Old English Epilogue plaints. As early as the fourth century Prudentius, in verses composed as a preface to his collected works, looks back on his life as old age approaches and sadly laments the vanity of this world.[4] In the fifth century Dracontius, at the end of a long didactic poem *Carmen de Laudibus Dei*, laments his own miseries and looks for the bliss of heaven after the unhappiness of his life on earth.[5] Eugenius laments the approach of old age in two poems.[6]

We have evidence that these Latin poets, all of whom wrote in the provinces of Spain, Africa and Gaul, were known to Anglo-Saxon scholars,[7] and there can be little doubt that the preoccupation of Old English poetry with the themes of old age, death and the brevity of earthly joys came from Latin example, and that in the Epilogue plaints we have a direct descendant of the Latin plaints, scholastic and autobiographical (in a conventional form). The lyric-elegies that we are concerned with are very different in form and spirit, but there are indications in some common elements of subject matter that

[1] Migne, *Patrologia Latina* lxxx. cols. 285–7 and 291–4.

[2] Migne, *Pat. Lat.* lxxx. cols. 294–6.

[3] Fr. Vollmer, *Monumenta Germaniæ historica, Auctores Antiquissimi* xiv. 235.

[4] Migne, *Pat. Lat.* lix. cols. 767–776.

[5] Fr. Vollmer *loc. cit.* 108–113.

[6] *ibid.* 243 f.

[7] See J. D. A. Ogilvie, *Books known to Anglo-Latin Writers from Aldhelm to Alcuin.*

they may spring ultimately from the same roots. It remains to try to trace the connexion.

What distinguishes these Old English lyric-elegies from any other genre of this early period is that they are 'studies of situation or emotion applied to imaginary and nameless persons who are detached from any definite associations of time or place'.[1] Even when, as in *The Wife's Lament*, there may originally have been a story setting, any events referred to remain vague and shadowy, viewed as it were from a distance in an attitude of reflective detachment. And in two passages in *Beowulf* we find similar conventions of elegiac expression, in the lament of the last survivor of his race (lines 2247–66), who contemplates the empty hall and remembers its former glories, and in the lament of the old man for his son (2444–62). The first of these is clearly an elegiac motif introduced for its own poetic interest, and the second, although it is occasioned by the grief of the old king Hreþel for the death of his son, is an elegiac evocation of such grief, not a description of it. The old man laments the death of his only son (while Hreþel had sons surviving), and he, too, contemplates the empty, windswept hall – 'the riders sleep, the warriors in their graves' – though it is not even clear why the death of his son should render the hall thus empty. It would seem that, as in the later elegies and lyrics of Middle English, it is the speaker's present mood and thought and external surroundings that are the main interest, and that these have become stylized into conventional motifs.

For the same conventional motifs appear in the Old Welsh elegies [2] associated with the name of Llywarch Hên,[3] and here

---

[1] N. Kershaw, *Anglo-Saxon and Norse Poems*, 6.

[2] The similarity was first pointed out by E. Sieper, *Die altenglische Elegie* (Strassburg 1915).

[3] Llywarch Hên was a sixth-century chieftain, but the poems survive only in MSS of the twelfth and fourteenth centuries, and probably derive ultimately from a ninth-century school of Welsh poets of the eastern district of Powys. See Ifor Williams, 'The Poems of Llywarch Hên', *Proceedings of the British Academy* xviii (1932); and Rachel Bromwich, 'The Character of the Early Welsh Tradition', in *Studies in Early British History*, ed. Nora K. Chadwick (Cambridge, 1954), 119 ff.

also there is the same combination of personal lament, 'nature' description and sententious gnomic statement as in the Old English elegies. In the *Llywarch Hên* poems, after a dialogue in which his son is urged to battle, we have a lament by Llywarch Hên ('the Old') for the death of this son (the last and best of his twenty-four sons), and a lament by the old man for his own lost youth and vigour. And in a series of stanzas which follow, closely similar in style, about Urien and the wars in the North, he laments over the ruined hall that was once the court of Urien: 'the hearth of Rheged is overrun with thorns, brambles and weeds [1] – there is desolation where once a jovial band of warriors feasted and made merry.' [2] And there follows a series of stanzas on the ruined hall of Cynddylan, lord of Powys, uttered by his sister Heledd as she bewails her own wretched fate, comparing her present lot with the happy days of old. In these Old Welsh elegies, as in the Old English, the speaker is usually in an outdoor setting, where the cold and harshness of winter reflect the bitterness of his (or her) sorrows and accentuate the suffering, or the contrast of summer and fair weather makes the misery more poignant. In several of them the voice of the cuckoo brings sorrow to the one who hears it. And although there is no example among extant Old English lyric-elegies of a lament of the old man for his lost youth and vigour, there is a reference to such a lament when Beowulf recounts to Hygelac how the aged Hroþgar would recite poetry to the company in the hall:

> hwilum eft ongan   eldo gebunden
> gomel guðwiga   gioguðe cwiðan,
> hildestrengo; hreþer inne weoll,
> þonne he wintrum frod   worn gemunde (2111–14)

Also, apart from these common motifs, there is some similarity of approach between the Welsh and English lyric-elegies. Both make use of strong contrast (often between the present state of the speaker and some happier state). And in the

---

[1] Cf. *The Wife's Lament* 31.
[2] Ifor Williams, *loc. cit.* 291.

Welsh elegies nature description, though stylistically abrupt, plays an important part in the elegiac theme,[1] since it mentions those features of his external surroundings which strike the senses of the speaker as affecting his state of mind or body. In the Old English elegies the nature description is less spontaneous and more conventional, but it is used in the same way. And, as in the Welsh poems, it is the sounds, as well as the sights of nature that affect the poet, especially the cries of birds.

Of particular interest is the fact that the cuckoo's voice brings sorrow to the one who hears it, in several of the Welsh elegies as in *The Seafarer*. The cuckoo has a sad voice also in *The Husband's Message*, but nowhere else, so far as is known, in the literature of this early period, whereas the cuckoo as the bird of summer is familiar in early poetry.[2] Sir Ifor Williams believes that the tradition of the cuckoo as a bird of lament had its origin in Old Welsh, suggested by the identification of its cry with the interrogative *cw* (pronounced coo) 'where?'. This identification, he claims, made the cuckoo's cry particularly apt as an elegiac motif ('My kinsmen are dead. Where are they?').[3] But, as Sieper pointed out,[4] the cuckoo as a bird of lament appears also in the folk-lore of some East European countries, and it may be a widespread tradition of ancient origin. Whatever the origin of the tradition, the very fact that the cuckoo as a bird of lament, which is so frequent a motif in Welsh elegy, appears nowhere else in the poetry of North-West Europe except in *The Seafarer* and *The Husband's Message* must add weight to the other parallels between early Welsh and English lyric-elegy.

The importance of these parallels for our purpose is not to establish direct influence of one upon the other. This is perhaps

[1] See K. Jackson, 'Incremental Repetition in Early Welsh *Englyn*', *Speculum* xvi, 304 ff, and *Early Celtic Nature Poetry*, 110 ff.

[2] Cf. *Guðlac* 744, and Alcuin's *Versus de Cuculo* and *Conflictus Veris et Hiemis*. In Snorri's list of poetic names for the months (*Skáldskaparmál*, chap. 78) the first summer month is *gauk-mánuðr*.

[3] 'Lectures on Early Welsh Poetry', *Dublin Institute for Advanced Studies* (1944). 11.

[4] *op. cit.* 70 ff.

unlikely, since the similarities, significant as they are, are less marked than the differences between the two traditions. Both strike off from what seem to be the same conventional topics, and to a certain extent they treat them in the same way, but the over-all result is quite different in form and spirit. The Welsh elegiac poet is more concerned with epigram and lyricism: the Old English poet with a more general reflective theme. The similarities between them would appear to derive from a common background, and that this background was a Celtic one, or at some stage subject to Celtic influence, seems indicated by the fact that those characteristics of treatment common to both (notably the use of strong contrast in emotional reference and the distinctive 'nature' poetry, already discussed) are much stronger in the Welsh than the English elegies, and more typical of Celtic poetry generally (both Welsh and Irish) than of poetry of the Germanic tradition. Also the gnomic accessories, which occur only sporadically in the English elegies, appear to be an almost indispensable ingredient of Old Welsh elegy. There seems to be ground, therefore, for supposing that, in some features at least, the Old English lyric-elegies are of 'Celtic inspiration'.[1]

There is also ground for supposing that this background of lyric-elegiac tradition from which the extant Old English and Old Welsh poems appear to derive their common features was itself a Christian background. It is difficult to explain otherwise the poetic pattern of reflective lament in which events are viewed in the perspective of moral or spiritual values, for the sententious gnomic statements usually have some relation to the elegiac lament, however abruptly they may be introduced, and often they are themselves, directly or indirectly, of Christian relevance. Moreover, the conventional themes of this lyric-elegiac poetry lend themselves by their very nature to the familiar early Christian preoccupation with death and decay and the insecurity of earthly happiness; and one of those themes – the lament of the old man for his youth – is a lyrical expression of what, in a more scholarly form, is the theme of

[1] See Nora K. Chadwick, in *The Heritage of Early Britain* 125.

the Epilogue plaints, and these, as we have seen, follow the example of the early Christian plaints. It seems unlikely that there were two separate and independent traditions of elegiac poetry, one scholastic and one lyrical, in which the old man laments his youth and broods on the death of friends and kin. More probably what Helen Waddell remarks of the lyric tradition of a later age – that it 'seems as new a miracle as the first crocus, but its earth is the leaf-drift of centuries of forgotten scholarship' [1] – applies in some measure also to this earlier lyric-elegiac tradition. Probably the familiar Christian theme of the brevity of earthly life and happiness found its way as part of a floating mass of ecclesiastical traditions into the repertoire of poets less learned than the early Christian Latin poets, and in the process the more picturesque and concrete aspects of the theme were selected and transmuted into poetic motifs that have become a part of the furniture of the lyric-elegiac poet.

Not all the conventional motifs, however, can be traced to the known homiletic reflections on mortality. The lament of the exile and contemplation of the ruined or empty hall have no place in those homiletic reflections. But it is probable that these motifs also derive from 'the leaf drift of forgotten scholarship'; and the literature of Gaul in the fifth and sixth centuries offers a possible place of origin, especially if the Celtic development of the genre preceded the English. Mrs N. K. Chadwick has shown in her study of poetry and letters in early Christian Gaul that there is evidence of more or less continuous intellectual contact between Gaul and the British Isles during this period, and conditions in Gaul then were such that its poets, who often describe in detail the contemporary scene, have occasion sometimes to refer to the exile of great landowners from their estates and the ruin of their ancestral homes. Descriptions of these things occur in the *Eucharistikon*, written by Paulinus of Pella in 459,[2] and in *De Redito Suo*, written by Rutilius Nama-

[1] *The Wandering Scholars* ix.
[2] Ed. and trans. by H. G. Evelyn White in the Appendix to his Loeb edition of *Ausonius*, 304 ff.

19

tianus *c.* 415, where he describes his return to his ruined home in Gaul, and laments as he looks upon it, and reflects upon the vast number of ruins that are increasing by neglect.[1] Venantius Fortunatus at the end of the sixth century, writing for his friend the Frankish queen Radegunde on the theme of her fallen dynasty, includes an elegiac description of the ruined hall of that dynasty.[2]

Of course, Gaul was not the only place to suffer from social disruption and devastation, but it is the fact that its poets describe these things that may be significant, since the conventional nature of the themes of exile and ruined halls in the Old Welsh and Old English elegies suggests a literary source. In some instances the poet may be describing a ruin at first hand, but the vogue of elegiac contemplation of ruins is likely to have literary authority. Moreover, the ruin theme in the Old Welsh elegies is always a part of the theme of exile, as it usually is in the Latin poems. It is the 'homeless wanderers', Llywarch and Heledd, who lament as they look upon the ruined halls of Urien and Cyndyllan, and it is as 'homeless wanderers' that Llywarch and Heledd are remembered in the Triads of the eleventh and twelfth centuries.[3] In the Old English *Wanderer* the connexion between the theme of the 'homeless wanderer' and the theme of the ruined hall has become a less integral one, but the juxtaposition of the two themes suggests that some connexion still persists. In *The Seafarer* the exile theme is wholly severed from the idea of banishment and the ruined hall, but the strong similarity to *The Wanderer* seems to indicate that its ultimate ancestry was the same.

How far the 'nature' poetry of this lyric-elegiac tradition also derives from the example of early Christian Latin literature is doubtful. Spontaneous and acute observation of the things of nature was a special gift of Celtic poets, but the

[1] See Mrs N. K. Chadwick, *Poetry and Letters in Early Christian Gaul* 124 and 127.

[2] See A. Brandl, 'Venantius Fortunatus und die ags. Elegien *Wanderer* und *Ruine*', *Archiv* cxxxix. 84.

[3] See Ifor Williams, 'The Poems of Llywarch Hên' 300.

particular use made of the gift in the Old Welsh elegies may have had as its starting-point the early Christian poet's use of natural phenomena as symbols or illustrations. For instance, the changing seasons are used to stress the inexorability of time or the inevitability of death. And that is true also of the Welsh elegies, and possibly of *The Seafarer* 48–55[a].

There is, however, one feature of *The Seafarer* which does not fit into this picture of the genesis of the lyric-elegy. Only in *The Wanderer* and *The Seafarer* is voyaging on the sea used as an elegiac motif in this genre. It is, however, used as a motif in another poem in the Exeter Book, *Resignation*.[1] But the relevant passage is obscure. The poem itself is a clumsy blend of the two types of Old English elegy. For the most part it is plaint and invocation of a type familiar in the Epilogue plaints, but the diction and imagery of lyric-elegy emerge in the figure of the exile (89[b]–96[a]) and the symbol of the growing tree (105–106[a]). In the first of these passages the speaker tells in the third person of the *anhoga . . . wineleas wrǣcca*, and from what follows, in the first person, it appears that he himself, eager to make a journey across the sea, has not the means to buy a boat. Mr E. G. Stanley suggests that it is the example of the *anhoga* which induces his own longing to make a pilgrimage.[2] If this is the correct interpretation it would seem that the 'homeless wanderer' has become identified with the voluntary Christian pilgrim who crosses the sea. But the passage might be interpreted metaphorically: the *anhoga . . . wineleas wrǣcca* might refer to man as an exile from Paradise, and the speaker's longing to make the sea-journey might be a longing to seek his heavenly home. Then the case for a similar metaphorical interpretation of *The Seafarer* would be strengthened, and it would appear that the ecclesiastical metaphor has found a vehicle in the lyric-elegiac genre. This does not mean that the process was merely one of 'secularization'.[3] For if lyric-elegy was itself an offshoot from the scholastic plaint it would be natural for a poet wishing to express the Christian doctrine that there is no

[1] See G. P. Krapp and E. V. K. Dobbie, *The Exeter Book* 215–18.
[2] *loc. cit.* 456–7.   [3] See G. V. Smithers, *loc. cit.* 151.

lasting hope in earthly happiness to begin his poem with a personal lament, and the theme of exile was probably already to hand in the tradition in which he is writing. The fact that 'exile' is also an ecclesiastical metaphor gives the theme a symbolic force, and it may have been the further metaphors of 'seafaring' as a symbol of man's life on earth that suggested the association of the theme of exile with seafaring. But the desolation of the wintry scene and the misery of the exile, though symbolically they become aspects of *erumna*, the 'hardship, misery' of man's lot in this world, are probably, in origin, the conventional motifs of the lyric-elegiac theme of the 'homeless wanderer'.

If this is the explanation of the genesis of the seafaring theme it does not entirely exclude the possibility that the poet was influenced also by the idea of the voluntary Christian pilgrimhermit. For once the 'homeless wanderer' of elegy is seen also as a symbolic figure of the *peregrinus* or 'alien' in this world, journeying to seek his heavenly home, his journeying becomes more purposeful. And it is not a far cry from the metaphorical *peregrinus* to the 'real' *peregrinus* making his real journey for the same purpose. But whether the poet himself made the connexion is difficult to determine, since the theme is cast so firmly in the mould of the conventional lament of the 'homeless wanderer'.

Still further literary influences have contributed to the making of *The Seafarer*. Like *The Wanderer*, in using the elegiac form for a homiletic purpose it follows to some extent the example of early Christian Latin elegy, and there is a special similarity in the later part of the poem to some poems written in Gaul in the sixth century. We may compare, for instance, lines 80–90 of *The Seafarer* and 92–5 of *The Wanderer* with lines written by Venantius Fortunatus on the brevity of earthly power and glory: *Tempora lapsa volant . . . Quid sunt arma viris? Cadit Hector et ultor Achilles*[1] . . . And still closer similarities to *The Seafarer* are to be found in Columbanus' *De Vanitate et Miseria Vitae Mortalis* and *Ad Hunaldum Epistola*. These poems contain a significant number of the ideas which appear in the

[1] Text and trans. in Helen Waddell's *Medieval Latin Lyrics* 66–7.

22

second half of *The Seafarer*: (i) the passing and failing of this world, as of every man's life, day by day; (ii) the brevity of earthly prosperity and well-being; (iii) the unknown day of death; (iv) the transitoriness of the power of kings and leaders; (v) the miseries of old age, with a description of the failings of the flesh; (vi) the uselessness of gold beyond the grave. All these themes are used as warning to reflect on mortality, and in *Ad Hunaldum Epistola* there is also a description of the changing of the seasons, illustrating the inexorability of time's passing, which may have some bearing on *The Seafarer* lines 48–52: when the signs of spring warn the Seafarer to make his journey, it is perhaps for the same reason.

It is unlikely, however, that these poems were the source of the second part of *The Seafarer*. For the same homiletic pattern, the warning to reflect on mortality, supported by the same ancillary themes, appears in some of the Old English homilies of the tenth century and later, which must have derived it from sources still closer to the form in which it appears in *The Seafarer*.[1] The clearest parallels are in pseudo-Wulfstan xxx,[2] pseudo-Wulfstan xlix,[3] and Bodley 343, no. 12.[4]

These homilies supply some further parallels to the homiletic ideas in *The Seafarer*, which do not appear in Columbanus' poems, notably that no man can save the sinful soul of another from Judgement (cf. *The Seafarer* 97–102 and 113–16), and

[1] See J. Cross, '*Ubi sunt* Passages in Old English – Sources and Relationships', *Vetenskaps-Societetens i Lund Årsbok* (1956) 25–44; and G. V. Smithers, *loc. cit.* 140–4.

[2] MS Hatton 113. See A. Napier, *Wulfstan's Homilies*: 143 ff (note especially 148).

[3] MSS Corpus Christi College Cambridge, 421 and 302, no. 33; also as Blickling Homily viii, and in Junius 85, both having lost most of their text through mutilation. See Napier, 250 ff (note especially 263). This homily appears in substantially the same form in the Vercelli collection no. x, and a relevant passage occurs in a separate version of the latter part in MSS CCCC 302, no. 12, and Cotton Faustina A ix, no. 6, collated by Assmann, *Bibliothek der Angelsächsischen Prosa* III, 164–9. There are parallels also in Blickling x.

[4] See A. O. Belfour, *Twelfth Century Homilies in MS Bodley 343*, E.E.T.S. (Original Series 137) 125 ff. (note especially 130).

they also offer some verbal parallels. The most significant of these concerns lines 80–8 of *The Seafarer*, which, as Mr Cross has shown, is a variant version of the motif which appears in these homilies (and in *The Wanderer*) in the form of a rhetorical question applied to the great ones of the past and their vanished glories: in all three homilies cited the words 'kings' and 'emperors' (*caseras*) are used, as in *The Seafarer* 82. And there are other verbal similarities: earthly prosperity is *wela* (cf. *eorþwelan*, *Seafarer* 67), and pomp and magnificence is *ofer-medla* (cf. *onmedlan*, *Seafarer* 81). The phrase *þeah þe* . . . is used frequently in admonitory passages, as in *The Seafarer* 97 and 113, and the phrase *Uton we*, as in *The Seafarer* 117, is typical of the final exhortation. The last two features are not, of course, confined to this particular homiletic pattern, but they help to establish the relation between *The Seafarer* and the Old English homilies, and in combination with the other similarities help to prove that *The Seafarer* derives its homiletic theme from the same, or a closely similar, source.

The ultimate sources of this homiletic pattern are to be found in passages from the Scriptures and the Fathers, but just where it assumed this more or less unified and conventional pattern is not known. One form of the lament for the great ones of the past appears under the heading *De Brevitate huius vite* in chapter lxxx of Defensor's *Liber Scintillarum*,[1] an anthology of passages from the Bible and patristic writings, compiled in the late seventh or early eighth century, with an interlinear gloss in Old English. Here the passage in question (*Dic ubi sunt reges? Ubi principes? Ubi imperatores?* . . .) is in a paragraph headed *Hieronimus dixit*, but, as Mr Cross has shown,[2] it is, in fact, from Isidore of Seville's *Synonyma de lamentatione animae peccatoris*,[3] Book II, paragraph 91, and the attribution to Jerome is probably due to a simple scribal error. The same passage from the *Synonyma* appears also, closely translated into Old English, in MS Cotton Tiberius A iii.[4]

[1] Ed. E. W. Rhodes, E.E.T.S. (Original Series 93) 1889.
[2] *loc. cit.* 25–7.   [3] Migne, lxxxiii. cols. 825 ff.
[4] Fol. 102 a. See F. Kluge, 'Nochmals der Seefahrer', *ESt* viii. 472 f.

Yet, as Mr Cross points out, there is not sufficient evidence for assuming that Isidore was the immediate source of the relevant passage in *The Seafarer* (lines 80–8). For though the context and the distinctive synonymous style (notably 'the kings, emperors and princes') mark it as deriving ultimately from the passage in the *Synonyma*, there is no rhetorical question, and there is the phrase *swylce iu wæron*, which has no parallel in the Isidore passage, but which appears again in a slightly variant form in pseudo-Wulfstan xlix as *þe jo wæron*, and also in two other Old English homilies, one which prefaces a list of instructions for the clergy (Thorpe's *Ecclesiastical Institutes*, 467) and an unpublished Old English homily, MS Cambridge University Library I i l. 33 pp. 409–17.[1] In the latter the homilist quotes in Latin as the words of S. Augustine: *O homo, dic mihi, ubi sunt reges, ubi sunt principes, ubi imperatores, qui fuerant ante nos . . .*

This attribution to Augustine is interesting in view of the fact that a version of the *ubi sunt* theme, somewhat different from that which appears in *Liber Scintillarum*, is contained in the Latin homily *Ad Fratres in Eremo* 68,[2] which is in a collection attributed in the early Middle Ages to Augustine. And this pseudo-Augustinian homily contains other material reproduced in *The Seafarer* and the three Old English homilies most nearly related to it; for instance, fighting against the devil (cf. *Seaf.* 76), and a brief contrast between youth and old age (cf. the fuller description of old age in *Seaf.* 91–6 and in pseudo-Wulfstan xxx). A variant version of *Ad Fratres* 68 also appears among the homilies formerly attributed to Isidore,[3] which is taken from a ninth-century MS. But neither of these Latin homilies is close enough to the second half of *The Seafarer* to be regarded as its source. There appears to have been another recension, different from any yet identified, which supplied the basis for the reflections on mortality in the Old English homilies, and probably it was this version that was known to the poet of *The Seafarer*. All the ideas it must have contained are to be found in popular patristic sources, chiefly those attributed

---

[1] Quoted by J. Cross, *loc. cit.* 33.　　[2] Migne, *Pat. Lat.* xl. cols. 1354–5.
[3] Migne, *Pat. Lat.* lxxxiii. cols. 1223–4.

in the early Middle Ages to Augustine and Isidore, and these ideas must at some stage have been assembled into a stylized pattern. Early Latin homiletic poems, such as Columbanus' *De Vanitate et Miseria Vitae Mortalis*, may have contributed to the process of stylization, and it is possible that, at a later stage, poems like *The Seafarer* helped to crystallize the homiletic ideas still further into the form in which they appear in the Old English homilies. It has been shown that style and diction of the earlier Old English homilies owe much to the familiar technique of Old English poetry,[1] and it may be that the debt was more than one of technique. Possibly it was in poems like *The Seafarer* that some of the Latin homilies first appeared in Old English form.

This might help to account for the fact that *The Seafarer* shows such freshness and apparent originality in its treatment of the homiletic theme. There is a remarkable freedom from clerical influence in its style and diction. Except in the direct Christian admonition at the end of the poem, the poet has transformed his homiletic material into terms and concepts which belong to a poetic milieu nearer to that of *Beowulf* than to the more stereotyped clerical school of poetry such as we have in the Cynewulfian poems. Both *The Wanderer* and *The Seafarer* are the work of poets to whom it is natural to use the terms of Germanic secular poetry to express their homiletic themes. The picture of the vanished life of the hall in *The Wanderer*, and the glories of the 'golden age' of the past in *The Seafarer* 80–90, though clearly derived from the homiletic *ubi sunt* motif, are expressed in a form that would have a special significance to an audience familiar with Germanic heroic poetry. And the process was evidently a conscious one, since the same tendency to exploit the terms of heroic poetry, though for a different purpose, is seen in the way in which the poet of *The Seafarer* plays upon the double meaning of certain words. As S. B. Greenfield has shown,[2] in lines 41ᵇ–43 the word *dryhten* is used in two distinct references to denote the lord–subject relationship, the social and the spiritual: 'There is no

---

[1] See R. Vleeskruyer, *The Life of St Chad* 19.
[2] 'Attitudes and Values in *The Seafarer*', *Studies in Philology* li. 18–20.

man on earth . . . whose (earthly) lord is so gracious to him
that he never has anxiety as to the fate the (heavenly) Lord
will assign him.' And similarly in lines 64ᵇ–88ᵃ the words
dream, *duguð* and *blæd* are used of the mutable joys and glories of
social life as contrasted with the eternal joys and glories of
heavenly life. And *lof*, the glory that is the praise of one's
fellows in line 73, becomes glory among the angels in line 78.
These double meanings were, of course, current in the language itself, but in underlining them thus the poet points the
contrast between the heroic and the Christian ideal.

This use of heroic tradition, whether for a didactic purpose
or as poetic background, is different from that of the writers of
Old English biblical epic, who tended to express their historic
subjects in terms of heroic poetry, sometimes with unfortunate
results. Unlike biblical narrative, elegy has a timeless quality
and is concerned with universal truths which may be expressed
in the guise of any tradition without incongruity. The mutability of earthly prosperity is just as truly illustrated by the
vanished joys typical of Germanic society as it is by the death
of Hector or Achilles, and to those familiar with Germanic
heroic poetry, more forcibly. We may even go so far as to say
that what gives *The Wanderer* and *The Seafarer* their enduring
poetic appeal is largely the fact that, while they are concerned
with the commonplaces of universal truths, their approach is an
oblique one. They give poetic reality to those commonplaces
by setting them in terms of personal experience, imaginative
and lyrical, against the background of an ancient poetic heritage.

DATE AND PLACE OF ORIGIN

The Exeter Book, in which the only extant text of *The Seafarer* is
preserved, has been assigned to the period 970–90, but as Dr
Sisam remarks: 'it is unlikely that the compilation was first
made in the Exeter Book, whose stately, even style indicates
that it was transcribed continuously from a collection already
made'.[1] Thus we may safely assume that *The Seafarer* was com-

[1] *Studies in the History of Old English Literature*, chap. 6, 'The Exeter Book', 97.

27

posed some time before the date of the MS – but how long before, and where, are more difficult questions.

We can trace its history back some little way in the history of the Exeter Book itself. Dr Sisam has shown that, whereas in the *Beowulf* MS 'every text is distinguished from the rest by the presence or absence or relative frequency of certain forms, and no really distinctive form runs through the collection', in the Exeter Book 'several forms are characteristic of the whole miscellany, and it is hard to be sure of any that distinguishes one text or group from another'. And he concludes that 'the *Beowulf* collection has, in the main, been mechanically copied from the time it was formed, while the Exeter collection has at some time been copied by one or more scribes who freely substituted forms to which they were accustomed for those in the copy before them'.[1] He considers it unlikely that the latest scribe is responsible, since he appears to have been a mechanical copyist. But the characteristic features are such as 'might possibly be found together, towards the middle of the tenth century, in the South-Western district where the Exeter Book itself was copied'.[2]

Among these features are:

(i) Forms with short *o* in stressed syllables before a nasal (*Seafarer*: *mon* 12 etc., *monað* 36, etc., *onmedlan* 81, *onsyn* 91). The other three poetical codices (*Beowulf*, Vercelli and Junius 11) have both *o* and *a* forms.

(ii) *hy*, *hi* forms (*Seafarer*: *hi* 84). As Dr Sisam remarks, *hi* was already common in the two MSS of the *Pastoral Care* that were written in Alfred's time. Evidently the other three poetical codices, where *hie* is more usual, were influenced by dialects where it remained throughout the tenth century.

(iii) The characteristic early West Saxon *ie* after a palatal *g* (*Seafarer*: *soðgied* 1, *gielleð* 62, *goldgiefan* 83, *forgiefene* 93), and sporadic *ie* forms from *i*-mutation (*Seafarer*: *stieran* 109). These *ie* forms are much more frequent in the Exeter Book than in the other three poetical codices, and there are indications that the scribe found *ie* spellings in his exemplar.

---

[1] *ibid.* 106.   [2] *ibid.* 102–3.

If these distinctive linguistic features were imposed on the text of the Exeter Book at some stage earlier than the extant copy it is likely to have been at a period when conditions favoured free rather than mechanical transcription, and this presumes a period when the copying of vernacular texts was an important, not a subsidiary, part of the scribe's work. Dr Sisam suggests from this argument that 'the whole miscellany was assembled in the time of Alfred, or his successors Edward and Athelstan, all of whom appreciated Old English poetry'.[1]

This would give us a date *c.* 940 as a *terminus ad quem* for the composition of *The Seafarer*. We must look to the poem itself for a *terminus a quo*, which is a more difficult problem, since the evidence is scanty and of uncertain value. For instance, it might be argued that the archaic spelling *u* for *w* in *huilpan* (21), and the consistent use of the *bi-* form of the unaccented prefix (in *bigeat* 6, *bidroren* 16, *bihongen* 17 and *bigeal* 24) may be indications that the text has been copied from an old exemplar. But *u* for *w* is not uncommon in late texts, especially in the combination *cu, hu*. And the *bi-* form of the verbal prefix, which also occurs sporadically in late texts, is usual in the *Vespasian Psalter Gloss*, which was written in Canterbury *c.* 870 and had its origin in the South-West Midlands.

The dating of the poem must to some extent depend on the interpretation we give to its subject matter, and here more recent research has brought a different view-point. Some commentators have thought that there is a reference to burying treasure with the dead, in lines 97–102, intended to discredit the heathen belief that the treasure may be taken into the next world; and similarly a reference to the heathen custom of cremation has been seen in lines 113–15. But the former passage is more probably a poetic expression of Christian ideas about the futility of lavish burial, and the latter a reference to the fire of hell (see notes to these lines). Thus there is nothing that can be regarded with certainty as evidence that *The Seafarer* belongs to an early period when such heathen beliefs were living

[1] *ibid.* 108.

enough to need discrediting. It has even been argued that the melancholy attitude and the narrowness of Christian outlook reflects a period of 'Frühchristentum', when men were struggling to accept the newer ideals of resignation to God's will in place of the older values.[1] But to regard this outlook as a mark of early date is to ignore the strong similarity to the homilies of the tenth century. The same Christian attitude appears also in homilies of the eleventh and twelfth centuries, and is to be found in some of the religious lyrics of the thirteenth.

We should bear these thirteenth-century lyrics in mind also with relevance to what might be regarded as other signs of immaturity in *The Seafarer* – the abrupt transitions of thought, and the simple, at times almost naïve, expression, compared, for instance, with the more logical, and lofty, dignified expression of the poems of Cynewulf. The difference is largely a difference of genre, and may have no relevance to dating. In adapting the technique of the poetry of entertainment to his homiletic purpose the poet of *The Seafarer* may have had in mind a less-educated listener. And there are some features in the language of the poem which point to a fairly late date. There is a tendency to long and involved sentences, with more use of subordinate clauses, and less use of parallelism than in the more traditional, Germanic style (e.g. lines 71–80ª). The deliberate play on the double meaning of certain terms (*blæd*, *lof*, *duguð*, etc.) argues a sophistication that is hardly likely at an early date. Also, if the suggested interpretation of lines 97–102 is right (see note) the use of the verb *willan* to express the future tense, with no notion of volition, is a syntactical feature that would not be natural until a fairly late period.

A more precise dating of the poem might be possible from its homiletic characteristics, if we knew more about the origins of the Old English homilies, because, although the actual homiletic source or sources may have been Latin, there are some distinctive features of phrasing which link it with the Old English homiletic tradition, e.g. the pattern *þæs* or *to þæs* + adj.

[1] See J. H. W. Rosteutscher, 'Germanischer Schicksalsglaube und angelsächsische Elegiendichtung', *ESt* lxxiii (1938). 1–31.

to express conditions of men or precepts of conduct, as in lines 39–41, and *þeah þe* to introduce a conditional admonition, as in lines 97 and 113. L. Vleeskruyer has shown that the Old English homiletic tradition, if it did not in fact originate in West Mercia, was probably transmitted to late Old English through West Mercian channels, and those Old English homilies in which the closest parallels to *The Seafarer* are to be found show signs of derivation from Mercian originals of the ninth century.[1]

This possible link with the West Mercian homiletic tradition of the ninth century is significant also in view of the fact that the Welsh lyric-elegies, to which *The Seafarer* appears to have some relation, have been assigned by some scholars to the early or mid-ninth century, and are thought to have been composed originally in the border regions of Shropshire and Hereford-shire, and to be the work, not of 'aristocratic' poets or clerics, but of a lower class, possibly retainers of local chieftains, in touch with popular traditions.[2] It seems probable that in the border area of mixed Welsh and English population, where there would probably be some bi-lingualism, especially at the lower social levels, English poets would learn something from the Welsh about the art of lyric poetry, in the same way as the Norse poets in Ireland learned from the Irish.

However that may be, it seems likely that such a feature as the cuckoo as a bird of lament comes from the same back-ground as the Welsh tradition, and so we have in the West Midland region of the mid-ninth century, and possibly a little earlier, an environment, both poetic and homiletic, in which *The Seafarer* might well have had its origin. But it is also true that when Wessex became a cultural centre, in Alfred's time, it, too, might have furnished the necessary conditions. There may have been some Welsh influence in Wessex then, through the agency of Asser and possibly other Welsh scholars, and, still more important, Alfred derived the greatest assistance in his literary activities from scholars who came from West Mercia. These scholars may well have brought with them a body of lyric-elegiac poetry, or the fashion of composing such

[1] *The Life of St Chad* 39–56.   [2] See Rachel Bromwich, *loc. cit.* 129.

poetry, as well as a familiarity with the West Mercian homiletic traditions. *The Ruin*, which belongs to the same, or a similar, school of poetry, is probably a description of the ruins of Bath and has been ascribed, though not conclusively, to Wessex.[1]

Not much can be found in the language of *The Seafarer* to support or refute these suggestions of its place of origin. The language is in the main that of the Exeter Book as a whole, i.e. predominantly West Saxon, with a number of Anglian forms (*calde* 8, *ælda* 77, *stregan* 97, *meotud* 103, etc.). It also uses consistently the uncontracted forms of the third singular present indicative (*limpeð* 13, *beodeð* 54, etc.), which have often been regarded as proof of Anglian origin, since they are forms that are confirmed by metre. But Dr Sisam has shown that there is no evidence that these forms are indications of dialectal origin: it would appear rather that 'the uncontracted forms were regarded as appropriate to verse, at least till the end of the tenth century, by writers for whom the short forms were normal in prose'.[2] Nor can the other Anglian forms in *The Seafarer* be regarded as evidence of an Anglian original, since the evidence of Old English poetry preserved in MSS of the late tenth or early eleventh centuries shows that there was a standard 'classical' or literary language of poetry, which was predominantly West Saxon with a strong Anglian element. Unless there is strong reason to suspect otherwise, therefore, the Anglian forms in a poetic text of this period must be attributed to the scribes who used this standard literary language. Only one form in *The Seafarer* gives ground for suspicion, and that is the form *tiddege* in line 69. Since *dæg* is the usual form in the poetic MSS of this period, *tiddege* might be thought to be a chance survival from a Mercian original, and the fact that it has been miscopied as *tide ge* as due to its unfamiliarity to a West Saxon scribe. But not much weight can be put on one form, itself an emendation.

[1] See C. A. Hotchner, *Wessex and Old English Poetry, with special consideration of The Ruin* (New York, 1939).

[2] 'The Dialect Origins of the earlier Old English Verse', *op. cit.* chapter 8, 125.

The Seafarer

(Exeter Book, fol. 81ᵇ–83ᵃ)

MÆg ic be me sylfum soðgied wrecan,
siþas secgan, hu ic geswincdagum
earfoðhwile oft þrowade,
bitre breostceare gebiden hæbbe,
5 gecunnad in ceole cearselda fela,
atol yþa gewealc, þær mec oft bigeat
nearo nihtwaco æt nacan stefnan,
þonne he be clifum cnossað. Calde geþrungen

Textual Variants: 6 *bigeat*: MS bigéat.

1] Cf. the opening of *The Wife's Lament*: *Ic þis giedd wrece bi me ful geomorre, minre sylfre sið; ic þæt secgan mæg hwæt ic yrmþa gebad.* N. Kershaw compares this use of *mæg* with that in the Lindisfarne Gospels, where *mæg* sometimes renders the Latin fut. indic.

2] *geswincdagum*: use of the dat. to give attendant circumstances, 'in days of hardship'.

5] *cearselda* occurs only here and means lit. 'abodes of sorrow'. Emendations have been suggested, to *cearsælða* (Ettmüller) and *cearsiða* (Klaeber, *JEGPh* xxiii. 124), on the ground that *seld*, a word properly denoting a human dwelling, could hardly be applied to the empty wastes of the sea. But the MS reading may be defended as an ironic metaphor: just as *meduseld* in *Beow.* is a place where mead is to be had, *cearseld* is a place where sorrow is to be had.

6] *atol yða gewealc* is in apposition to *cearselda fela*; *yða gewealc* is a common designation for the sea, and this same half-line occurs in *Exodus* 456.

bigeat: an unusual use of *bigietan* with an emotional connotation to describe a circumstance or state of mind taking hold of, and affecting, a person; cf. *The Wife's Lament* 32: *ful oft mec her wraþe begeat fromsiþ frean*, and 41: *. . . longaþes þe mec on þissum life begeat.*

8] *cnossað*: the change to the present tense is probably to mark the habitual nature of the action; cf. *Beow.* 1923. *Cnossian*, intrans., occurs only here, and probably has a different meaning from the trans. *cnyssan*, 'beat upon, strike'. Translate 'dashes by the cliffs', rather than 'strikes on the rocks' (BT).

33

wæron mine fet,   forste gebunden
10 caldum clommum,   þær þa ceare seofedun
   hat' ymb heortan;   hungor innan slat
   merewerges mod.   Þæt se mon ne wat
   þe him on foldan   fægrost limpeð,
   hu ic earmcearig   iscealdne sæ
15 winter wunade   wræccan lastum,
   †winemægum bidroren,

14 *sæ*: MS sǽ.

9] *wæron mine fet*: emended by Sweet to *wæron fet mine* for metrical reasons, since the alliteration is on *f*, and although the second lift alone may alliterate in the first half-line, it usually does so only when the first lift is a less strongly accented word, whereas adjs. preceding their nouns normally bear the stronger stress. With *min*, however, the usage varies; cf. *Beow.* 262, 410, etc., for examples of *min* preceding its noun in the first half-line, without bearing the alliteration.

11] *hat* (MS) is emended in some editions to *hate*, to agree with *ceare* – unnecessarily, however, since the final *-e* could be omitted through elision before *ymb*; cf. *bitter* 55, and *Beow.* 338, 668, 2600, etc. Surges of feeling were traditionally hot; cf. the use of *seoðan* and *wylm* in emotional application, frequently to denote grieving. There is a deliberate antithesis here between the hot sorrows within the heart and the physical cold afflicting the body.

hungor may imply more than its literal meaning here and include figuratively the pangs of loneliness and suffering that gnaw at the Seafarer's heart.

12] *merewerges*; adj. used as subst., 'one weary of (or because of) the sea'. *Werig* usually denotes a greater degree of suffering than is generally implied by its modern derivative.

13] *þe him . . . limpeð*: lit. 'whom it befalls in fairest manner on land', i.e. 'whose lot is cast most happily on land'. Cf. *Gen.* 157: *stod bewrigen folde mid flode*, where *folde* = '(dry) land'. Since *folde*, especially in the phrase *on foldan* is often used of the world in general, however, the Seafarer may be comparing his lot, not specifically with those fortunate enough to be on land, but with fortunate ones in the world generally.

14] *earmcearig* occurs only here and in *Wand.* 20. Unlike the usual OE compounds of noun + adj., it consists of two adjs. and the exact force of the combination is uncertain. Translate either 'wretched and sorrowful', or 'sorrowful because of my wretched state' (cf. *hwæteadig, Elene* 1194, which probably means 'successful because valiant').

16] There is no lacuna in the MS, and we have insufficient evidence of the practice of OE verse to know with certainty whether any of these instances of simple half-lines are intentional or due to scribal omission. But in view of the many errors in this text accidental omission seems more probable

bihongen hrimgicelum;   hægl scurum fleag.
Þær ic ne gehyrde   butan hlimman sæ,
iscaldne wæg.   Hwilum ylfete song
20 dyde ic me to gomene,   ganetes hleoþor
ond huilpan sweg   fore hleahtor wera,
mæw singende   fore medodrince.
Stormas þær stanclifu beotan,   þær him stearn oncwæð

---

18 *hlimman sæ*: MS hlimmán sǽ.

---

here. Ettmüller takes *winemægum bidroren* as the second half-line and
supplies *wynnum biloren* as the first. Rhyme, however, is not a characteristic
of *The Seafarer* or the poems most nearly related to it.

17] *hrimgicelum*: the only instance of this compound, which apparently
means much the same as *is-gicel*, mod. 'icicle'.

19ᵇ f] These lines modify the statement that nothing could be heard but
the roaring of the sea (18–19ᵃ). Some editors put a comma after *wæg* and a
stop after *song*, but more probably the change of sense and construction
comes, as often in OE poetry, in the middle of the line: 'At times the song of
the swan I had as my entertainment, the cry of the gannet and the voice of
the curlew instead of the laughter of men . . .' As Mrs Goldsmith remarks in
her study of the sea-birds in this passage (*RES* v. 225 ff), we cannot identify
all the species exactly, since from the evidence of glosses it appears that the
Anglo-Saxons did not make the clear distinctions between the species that are
made now. But she finds nothing to indicate that the poet did not know well
the habits and the cries of the birds he mentions. *ylfete song* clearly refers to the
cry of the whooper swan, which visits our coasts in winter, and the gannet
similarly often remains all the year. Mrs Goldsmith informs us that, though its
hoarse cry is usually heard only in the breeding season, it may sometimes be
heard in winter when the birds are excited over competition for a shoal of fish.

21] *huilpan*: an example of archaic *u = w*, though the spelling is not confined to early texts, especially in the combination *hu, cu*. Miss Daunt (*MLR*
xiii. 478) and Miss Kershaw would identify the bird as the bar-tailed godwit
or 'yarwhelp'. But both the mod. English and Scottish dialect *whaup* and the
cognate Low German forms, such as Dutch *wulp*, Frisian *wilp*, are used of
the curlew (see *NED* s. whaup), and this is pretty clearly the generic sense,
the godwit being called 'yarwhelp' because it resembles the curlew. Many
curlews are summer visitors only, but there are always some that remain
round our coasts in winter.

22] *medodrince*, usually translated 'drinking of mead', probably means, as
O. S. Anderson suggests, the drink itself 'mead', just as *windrinc* or *windrenc*
means 'wine'.

23] *Stormas þær stanclifu beotan* is a 'swollen' half-line with definitely three
beats. In view of the difficulty of translating *þæt* in the following line (see

isigfeþera;　ful oft þæt earn bigeal,
25†urigfeþra;　nænig hleomæga
　　feasceaftig ferð　frefran meahte.

26 *frefran* (Grein): MS feran.

---

below), it is worth noting that *storm stanclif beot* would be a normal half-line, and the change to the plural is just the sort of liberty a scribe might take with his text.

stearn is etymologically a variant of modern 'tern', which is still known in Norfolk dialect as *starn* (*EDD*). The name 'tern' is of Scand. origin, but of later date than the Danish invasions since the ON form is *þerna*, which later became Danish *terne*, Swedish *tärna*; (for the relation of *þerna* to *stearn*, cf. ON *þjórr* OE *steor* 'steer'). Whether *stearn* necessarily designates the same species of bird as mod. 'tern', however, is uncertain. *Stearn* is recorded elsewhere only in glosses where, in the forms *stærn*, *stern* and *stearn*, it glosses several Latin bird-names, including *sturnus* 'starling' (obviously by confusion with OE *stær* 'starling'). Since terns do not usually haunt cliffs and do not remain round our coasts in winter, Mrs Goldsmith is of the opinion that *stearn* was used not only of the tern or 'sea-swallow' but also of the smaller and more elegant of the gulls, such as the kittiwake.

oncwæð probably implies that the voice of the bird is heard between the crashing of the waves on the rocks, as if 'answering' them.

24] *þæt earn bigeal*: the reference of *þæt* is uncertain: it may refer back to the call of the *stearn* ('cried in answer to it'), or it may refer to the *stanclif* ('cried around the rocky cliff'; see note to 23), or, as Anderson suggests, *bigeal* may have the meaning 'screamed at, cried out against', and the whole phrase may describe the eagle screaming in protest at the storm. The *earn* here must be the sea-eagle, which was commonly known around our coasts in earlier days. It has a high reiterating call, whereas the golden eagle is usually silent.

25] This line lacks alliteration and no decisively convincing emendation offers itself. Thorpe assumes a loss of two half-lines between *urigfeþra* and *nænig hleomæga*. Grein substitutes *ne ænig* for *nænig* to supply vowel alliteration, and Holthausen (*Anglia Beibl* xix. 248) transposes the neg. to a position immediately before the verb. Kluge emends *urigfeþra* to *heaswigfeþra* 'dark-feathered', and the fact that *urigfeþra* is always applied to eagles (e.g. *Judith* 210, *Elene* 29, 111) is a point in favour of emending it, since a copyist might well have substituted a more conventional eagle adj. for a less familiar one. But as Mrs Goldsmith remarks, it is not only the alliterative break, but also the unfortunate echoing of *isigfeþera* in the preceding line that is suspicious, and she would prefer to emend to *hyrnednebba* 'horny-beaked', which is applied to the eagle in *Judith* 212.

26] *frefran* (*feran* MS). The emendation (Grein) is acceptable as giving good sense and being well within the range of scribal blundering. Cf. *Wand.* 28 for parallel use of *frefran*.

36

For þon him gelyfeð lyt,   se þe ah lifes wyn
gebiden in burgum,   bealosiþa hwon,
wlonc ond wingal,   hu ic werig oft
30   in brimlade   bidan sceolde.
Nap nihtscua,   norþan sniwde,
hrim hrusan bond,   hægl feol on eorþan,
corna caldast.   For þon cnyssað nu

---

33 *nu*: MS nú.

27] *For þon*: the normal meaning of this conjunctive phrase is 'for that reason' (either adverbial 'therefore', or conjunctive 'because'), but in some contexts in OE poetry, as here, it appears to be used in a more colourless sense as an introductory adverb to mark a shift of thought, and may be translated 'truly', 'indeed'. W. W. Lawrence, who first established the probability of this usage (*JEGPh* iv. 463) pointed out that in the Lindisfarne and Rushworth Gospels *for ðon* is used to gloss *quippe* or *vero* where the West Saxon version has *soðlice*. The difficulty of translating *for þon* in *The Seafarer* has been exaggerated, however. For instance, it has been claimed that it has the usual causal meaning in 72, 103 and 108, and an adversative meaning 'and yet' in 27, 33, 39 and 58. But, apart from the awkwardness of translating the phrase in two such divergent senses in one poem, there is no reason why *for þon* should not bear the normal causal sense in 33, 39 and 58: see notes to these lines.

28] *gebiden* is emended by Sweet and others to *gebideð*, and the scribal error could easily be explained by the fact that both the preceding and the following words end in -*n*. Miss Kershaw points out, however, that *ah* is used (like *hafað*) with the p.pt. in Wulfstan's *Address to the English* Sweet's *Anglo-Saxon Reader*,[11] (1948) p. 84, l. 56, and the same usage is found in the OHG *Ludwigslied* 24. Probably the construction retained a more literal force than with *hafað*, and we may translate: 'he who has a pleasant life, lived in dwellings of men, free from dangerous adventures (or hardships)', (*hwon* having, as often, an adverbial force).

in burgum. From the Laws of Alfred (cap. 40, cited by Miss Kershaw) it appears that *burh* was used of the dwelling of any man above the rank of peasant.

29] *wlonc ond wingal*: cf. *Ruin* 35, where the phrase is also applied to men in a *burh*. It was evidently an alliterative formula and need not imply any disapprobation.

31] Cf. *Wand.* 102–5 and *Beow.* 547.

33] *corna caldast*: a description of hail which probably goes back to common Germanic tradition. Cf. the Old Norwegian *Rune Song* 7: *Hagall er kaldastr korna,* and the OE *Runic Poem* 25: *Hægl byþ hwitust corna.*

33b–35] 'And so the thoughts trouble my heart now that I myself am to

37

heortan geþohtas   þæt ic hean streamas,
35 sealtyþa gelac   sylf cunnige –
    monað modes lust   mæla gehwylce
    ferð to feran,   þæt ic feor heonan
    elþeodigra   eard gesece –
    for þon nis þæs modwlonc   mon ofer eorþan,
40 ne his gifena þæs god,   ne in geoguþe to þæs hwæt,
    ne in his dædum to þæs deor,   ne him his dryhten
    to þæs hold,

---

venture on the deep (or towering) seas.' Evidently the voyage contemplated
is of a different kind from the experiences of seafaring already described.
See Introduction, p. 3 ff.

hean streamas: cf. *ofer heanne holm, Wand.* 82. It is tempting to translate this
'the high seas', but the meaning is probably rather different from the
modern idiom, which appears to have been influenced by analogy with
'high-road', 'high seat', etc., where 'high' originally had the sense 'main',
'chief'. In such expressions in OE, however, *heah* remains undeclined. *hean
streamas* probably means 'seas towering high' (cf. *holm*) or 'deep seas' (cf. *se
pytt heh is*, Lindisfarne Gospels, *John* iv. 11, where the West Saxon has *deop*).

37] *Ferð* (a frequent form for *ferhð*) may be the object of *monað*, or the
subject, parallel with *modes lust*. In l.53 *monað* is used without an object, either
absolutely or with the object (me) understood.

38] *elþeodigra eard*. This has usually been understood to refer to a foreign
land. But *elþeodig* means also 'one who sojourns as an alien, *peregrinus*' (BT
s.v). As G. V. Smithers has shown, it is applied in ecclesiastical writings to
good Christians who are 'aliens' in this world (see Introduction, p. 5).
elþeodigra eard, then is probably the (heavenly) home of *peregrini*.

39] *for þon* here is taken as loosely correlative with *For þon* of 33: the
thought of venturing across the sea troubles the Seafarer's heart *because* there
is no man, however fortunate, who does not have fears on his sea-voyage
about the fate the Lord may assign him. Lines 36–8, then, are in paren-
thesis.

40] *gifena . . . god* may mean either 'generous of gifts' or 'good in moral
qualities' (i.e. with *gifu* used in a fig. sense) but since the emphasis seems to
be on attributes of worldly success, the former interpretation seems preferable.

41] *his dryhten* for similar reasons appears to be his earthly lord, distinct
from *Dryhten* without qualifier in 43. The repetition is probably a deliberate
play on the word; see Introduction, p. 26. The construction is loose, but
less difficult syntactically than it would be in mod. English, since each circumstance or quality cited is equivalent to a relative clause (*nis mon* [*þe is*]
þæs modwlonc, ne [*þe is*] *. . ., ne* [*þe*] *him his dryhten* [*is*] *to þæs hold*), in which the

þæt he a his sæfore   sorge næbbe,
to hwon hine Dryhten   gedon wille.
Ne biþ him to hearpan hyge   ne to hringþege –
45 ne to wife wyn   ne to worulde hyht –
ne ymbe owiht elles   nefne ymb yða gewealc;
ac a hafað longunge   se þe on lagu fundað.
Bearwas blostmum nimað,   byrig fægriað,

42 *sæfore*: MS *sǽ fore*.

---

indeclinable *þe* would remain the same throughout, the change from nom. to dat. being indicated by *him*. Both *þæs* and *to þæs* were commonly used as adverbs of degree.

42 *sǽ fore* (gen.) *sorge*: 'anxiety on (or concerning) his voyage'.

43] Lit. '[as to] what the Lord will bring him to'. The sense of *gedon to* is 'bring into a condition' or 'put to a purpose'; cf. *gedon to nahte* 'bring to naught', or *gedon to deaðe* 'put to death'. In these lines (39–43) the poet has adapted to his seafaring theme a thought frequently expressed in Christian homily, that there is no man on earth, however fortunate, who does not have to face death; cf. *Wulfstan's Homilies* (Napier, p. 149, l. 17): *nis nan man swa rice on eorðan and swa mihtig and mære, þæt he ne sceole deaðes abyrgean*. But the wording of line 43 seems also to imply a reference to the fate of the soul after death; cf. *Admonition to Christian Life* 59 f: *Uncuð bið þe to hwan þin Drihten gedon wille*.

44–6] This is a passage which has often been misunderstood as meaning that the Seafarer has no pleasure in anything but the sea (see Introduction, p. 3). But *ymbe* and *ymb* of 46 can hardly be construed with *wyn* or *hyht* of 45; they must refer back to *hyge* of 44, and the intervening line is best understood as a parenthetic extension of the train of thought fired by *to hearpan hyge*: 'His thought is not on the harp nor on the receiving of rings; nor is his pleasure in woman nor his joy in worldly things; nor [is his thought] about anything else except the rolling of the waves.' Just as the related verb *hycgan* can be construed with either *to* or *ymb* (*to* implying thought for some specific object, *ymb* more general reflection) so here *hyge* is followed by *to* in 44 and *ymb(e)* in 46.

47] *longunge*: the context makes it clear that this does not mean a longing for the sea. *Longung* is often used of weariness of mind or distress, and Miss Kershaw's rendering, 'There is never any peace of mind for him who goes to sea', probably expresses well the literal sense, though there may be an underlying Christian significance of 'yearning' (see Introduction, p. 7).

48] *nimað* is not elsewhere construed with the dat. or instr., and it has been suggested that *blostmum* is an error for *blostman* possibly depending on ONorth *blostmu*, or that the phrase derives from a literal translation of Latin (cf. *foliis sese induit arbor* in Pentadius, *De Adventu Veris*). The construction,

wongas wlitigað,   woruld onetteð;
50 ealle þa gemoniað   modes fusne
   sefan to siþe   þam þe swa þenceð
   on flodwegas   feor gewitan.
   Swylce geac monað   geomran reorde;
   singeð sumeres weard,   sorge beodeð
55 bitter' in breosthord   Þæt se beorn ne wat,
   sefteadig secg,   hwæt þa sume dreogað

---

52 *gewitan* (Thorpe): MS gewitað.   56 *sefteadig* (Grein): MS eft eadig.

---

however, is parallel to that of *fon* with the dat.; cf. *Beow.* 2989: *He þam frætwum feng.*

fægrið may be intrans. here, with *byrig* as subject, 'the dwellings (or villages) grow fair'. E. Ekwall suggests (*Anglia Beibl* xxxv. 135), on the analogy of such verbs as *blacian, fulian, heardian*, etc., that this was the original usage. But in its only other occurrence *fægrian* is trans. 'to adorn' (see BT Suppl), and with *bearwas* as subject this gives good sense, 'adorn the dwellings'.

49] *wlitigað* is usually emended to *wlitigað*, but, as Dr Whitelock points out (*loc. cit.* 265), -*ig*- is a perfectly defensible spelling for [*iji*]. *Wlitigian*, like *fægrian*, is trans. in its other occurrences, and *wongas*, therefore, is probably the object, 'make beautiful the meadows'.

50–2] *sefan* is parallel to *fusne*: 'All these things urge [the man] eager of spirit, [urge] the heart to the journey, in one who thinks to venture far on the paths of the sea'.

gewitan: if the MS *gewitað* is retained, this line forms a separate sentence: 'they depart far over the paths of the sea'. But the sudden plural would be unnatural, and single lines forming a complete sentence are rare in OE verse. With the emendation, which is generally accepted, the line is reminiscent of *Beow.* 42: *on flodes æht feor gewitan.*

flodwegas may be either 'paths of the sea' or the Anglian form of *flodwægas* 'waves of the sea'. Cf. *Wand.* 46.

53] For the tradition of the cuckoo as a bird of lament see Introduction, p. 17.

54] *sumeres weard*: 'watchman' or 'guardian', or perhaps 'lord' of summer; cf. *wudubearwes weard* of the Phoenix (152).

55] *bitter* is either the fem. sg. accus. agreeing with *sorge* (i.e. *bittere* with final -*e* omitted because it is elided) or possibly the neuter used as a noun, 'bitterness' or 'a bitter fate'.

in breosthord: the accus. with *in* is used naturally of sorrow to come *into* his heart.

56] *sefteadig* (*efteadig* MS clearly, though some editions give the MS reading as *esteadig*). Grein's emendation to *sefteadig* is preferable to *esteadig*

þe þa wræclastas   widost lecgað.

    For þon nu min hyge hweorfeð   ofer hreþerlocan,
min modsefa   mid mereflode,
60 ofer hwæles eþel   hweorfeð wide,
eorþan sceatas,   cymeð eft to me
gifre ond grædig;   gielleð anfloga,

---

58 *nu*: MS nú.

---

metrically, since lines of this type (Siever's E-type) in the first half line usually have two alliterating staves. A compound of *eadig* with an adj. as in the assumed *sefteadig* can be paralleled in *hwæteadig*, *Elene* 1194.

þa sume: *sume* here is probably generic, not partitive; it denotes a certain class of people, defined in the following line: 'what those suffer who lay the tracks of exile to the farthest bound'.

58] *For þon*: this is one of the passages where *for þon* can hardly be translated 'therefore', and has been taken by Miss Daunt and others in an adversative sense, 'and yet'. But the difficulty disappears if we take *For þon* here as correlative with *for þon* as the conjunction in 64. Only the conjunction need be translated in modern idiom. The general sense of the passage, then, is that the Seafarer's spirit is impelled to traverse the ocean *because* the 'joys of the Lord' mean more to him than 'life on land'; see note to 64ᵇ–66ᵃ.

58–62ᵃ] G. V. Smithers regards it as 'a singular thing in OE poetry that *hyge* should be represented as ranging far abroad from the human being in whom it is normally lodged' (*Medium Ævum* xxvi. 137). But it was not unusual in OE poetry for *hyge*, *modsefa* or their poetic equivalents to be imagined as separable entities (*hyge wæs him hinfus*, *Beow.* 755), and even as being sent over the sea (cf. *Wand.* 55–7). Here the poet elaborates the concept: the Seafarer's spirit passes beyond the confines of his breast and returns to him again, eager and hungering (to be gone in reality).

eorþan sceatas cannot be taken as directly dependent on *hweorfeð*, since *hweorfan* is an intrans. verb, not used with the accus. of the space traversed. N. Kershaw takes *sceatas* as gen. sg. dependent on *wide* (cf. *wide landes*, BT Suppl s. *wide*). But there seems no reason why *eorþan sceatas* should not be an amplification of *hwæles eþel* in the preceding line: '. . . journeys widely over the haunt of the whale, (over) the expanse of the world'.

62ᵇ] *anfloga* is almost certainly, as Sieper suggests, the cuckoo. Some have understood it to be the spirit (*hyge*) sweeping over the sea like a bird; but the emphasis on the cries, which could have little or no metaphorical significance, would make such an image almost absurd. Others have understood it to be a seagull; but the seagull is not a 'lone-flier' as the cuckoo almost always is, and there has been no previous mention of a sea-bird to connect with the *anfloga*, whereas the cuckoo earlier incited him to the journey as the *anfloga* incites him now. Probably the passage is intended to mark the return

41

hweteð on hwælweg   hreþer unwearnum
ofer holma gelagu,   for þon me hatran sind
65 Dryhtnes dreamas   þonne þis deade lif
læne on londe.

Ic gelyfe no
þæt him eorðwelan   ece stondað.
Simle þreora sum   þinga gehwylce

---

63 *hwælweg* (Thorpe): MS wæl weg.   67 *stondað* (Ettmüller): MS stondeð.

---

to reality: when his spirit comes back to him again the Seafarer awakes to
consciousness of his surroundings and hears again the cuckoo's cry.

63] *hwælweg* (*wæl weg* MS). G. V. Smithers rejects the (usual) emendation
as 'palpably hazardous even by the ostensibly decisive metrical criterion'
(that a verb does not alliterate in preference to a noun in the first half-line).
Yet an emendation based on normal metrical practice is hardly very hazardous in a text by no means perfect, even when that metrical norm is shown to
be not invariable. And the parallels he produces in support of *wælweg*, as
meaning 'road taken by the dead' or 'road to the abode of the dead' are not
convincing. *Wæl*, usually used of the slain, is not the word one would expect
in such a context, and his parallels deriving from Norse mythology of the
Viking Age are of doubtful value as clues to Anglo-Saxon concepts. Even
the 'remarkable native parallel' *neosiþ*, recorded in *Vainglory* 55, is less
certainly a parallel than it may seem, since *siþ*, especially in compounds,
often indicates 'lot, condition' rather than 'journey': *neosiþ* therefore may
mean merely 'the condition of being a corpse', i.e. 'death'. The general sense
of the imagery as well as the metre favour the emendation to *hwælweg*.

64ᵇ-66ᵃ] 'for the joys of the Lord are warmer (more living or inspiring)
to me than this dead, transitory life on land'. *Dryhtnes dreamas* is a conventional expression for the heavenly life, and *hatran* is clearly opposed to *deade*,
used paradoxically with *lif* to denote worldly life, the life that is no life: i.e.
earthly happiness, epitomized for the Seafarer as life on land, is sterile and
fleeting, less living to him than the joys of heavenly life. For a discussion of this
passage in relation to the seafaring theme as a whole see Introduction, p. 4 ff.

67] There is no clear antecedent to *him*. It may refer loosely to one who
lives *þis deade lif*, *læne on londe*, or it may be used reflexively with *stondað* in the
sense 'endures'.

68-9] The best emendation of the meaningless *tide ge* of the MS is *tiddege*,
the Mercian form for *tiddæge* (Grein); cf. *Gen.* 1165, *ða his tiddæge . . . rim wæs
gefylled*, where *tiddæge* means 'span of life' with a connotation of 'final hour'
(*þa he woruld ofgeaf*). Therefore *tiddege* here probably refers to the end of the
span of life. Translate: 'Ever, in all conditions, one of three things hangs in
the balance until his final hour' (*his* referring either to mortal man generally
or to *fægum* of l. 71). The thought and expression of these and the following

42

ær his tiddege   to tweon weorþeð:
70 adl oþþe yldo   oþþe ecghete
fægum fromweardum   feorh oðþringeð.
For þon biþ eorla gehwam   æftercweþendra
lof lifgendra   lastworda betst,
þæt he gewyrce,   ær he on weg scyle,
75 fremum on foldan   wið feonda niþ,
deorum dædum   deofle togeanes,
þæt hine ælda bearn   æfter hergen,
ond his lof siþþan   lifge mid englum
awa to ealdre,   ecan lifes blæd,
80 dream mid dugeþum.

              Dagas sind gewitene,

---

69 *tiddege* (Grein *tiddæge*): MS tide ge.
71 *feorh*: MS fᵉorh.
72 *biþ*: MS þæt.
75 *fremum* (Sisam): MS fremman.
79 *blæd* (Thorpe): MS blæð.

---

two lines is similar to that of Hroþgar's 'sermon' to Beowulf, see especially
1735-9 and 1763-8, where *adl, ecg* and *atol yldo* are cited as possible occasions
of death to a man.

72-80ᵃ] The poet follows what was a familiar train of thought in both OE
and ON poetry in passing from the inevitability of death (70-1) to the idea
that fame after death, therefore, is best for a man (cf. *Beow.* 1386-9, and
Hávamál stanzas 76-7). He then relates the idea to his Christian theme, in an
involved sentence, with a play on the two meanings of the word *lof*, (i) the
praise expressed by a person, and (ii) the praise ascribed to a person, which
in Christian contexts was often applied to glory in heaven. If we emend *þæt*
(MS) of 72 to *biþ*, and the awkward inf. *fremman* (MS) of 75 to *fremum*
(Sisam, *ESt* xlvi. 336), we may translate: 'Therefore for every man the praise
of those who live after him and commemorate him is the best memorial,
which he may earn, before he must depart, by good actions on earth against
the wickedness of enemies (or fiends), opposing the devil with noble deeds,
so that the children of men will praise him afterwards and his glory will live
then among the angels for ever, [in the] blessedness of eternal life, bliss
among the noblest.' (The last two phrases are parallel to *lof*, amplifying and
explaining it.)

80-90] This eloquent lament for the golden age of the past is no doubt
intended as a reminder of the mutability of earthly glory in contrast to the
eternal glory described in the preceding lines. It is, in fact, a poetic para-
phrase of a theme which appears in several of the OE homilies (see

ealle onmedlan   eorþan rices;
nearon nu cyningas   ne caseras
ne goldgiefan   swylce iu wæron,
þonne hi mæst mid him   mærþa gefremedon
85 ond on dryhtlicestum   dome lifdon.
Gedroren is þeos duguð eal,   dreamas sind gewitene;
wuniað þa wacran   ond þas woruld healdaþ,
brucað þurh bisgo.   Blæd is gehnæged,
eorþan indryhto   ealdað ond searað,
90 swa nu monna gehwylc   geond middangeard.
Yldo him on fareð,   onsyn blacað,
gomelfeax gnornað,   wat his iuwine,
æþelinga bearn   eorþan forgiefene.
Ne mæg him þonne se flæschoma,   þonne him þæt
      feorg losað,
95 ne swete forswelgan   ne sar gefelan
ne hond onhreran   ne mid hyge þencan.

---

82 *nearon* (Grein): MS nǣron.

Introduction, p. 24), often taking the form of a rhetorical question; cf. Napier, *Wulfstan's Homilies* 263: *Hwær syndon nu þa rican caseras and þa cyningas þe jo wæron . . . hwær is heora ofermedla?* Cf. also *Wand.* 92–5.

82] *nearon; næron* (MS) is probably a scribal error due to the proximity of *wæron* in the next line.

84] *mid him*: 'among themselves', in mod. idiom 'between them'.

87] *wacran.* OE *wac* differed in meaning from its cognate ON *veikr*, from which mod. English *weak* is descended: *wac* meant primarily 'not firm', 'pliant', rather than 'not strong', and is often used in the sense 'wanting in moral firmness', and in the compar. 'degenerate' or 'inferior'. Cf. Napier, *Wulfstan's Homilies*, 83: *Hit is on worulde a swa leng swa wacre*; *men syndon swicole and woruld is þe wyrse.*

88] *brucað þurh bisgo*: 'occupy it in toil and trouble'. *Þurh* with an abstract noun is a frequent method of expressing the adverbial of manner or state (see BT s.v. III (6)).

91] *Yldo him on fareð*: *on* is adverbial and bears the allit. If this were an instance of inverted prep. it would be *hine on fareð.*

93] *forgiefene*: since *iuwine* may, historically, be the pl. form, the emendation to *forgiefenne* of some editors is unnecessary.

94] *feorg*: a later spelling for *feorh.* Since final *g* in such words as *beag* became unvoiced in late OE to *h*, spelt sometimes *h* and sometimes *g*, *g* tended to be used as a variant spelling for *h* after a back sound.

Þeah þe græf wille   golde stregan
broþor his geborenum,   byrgan be deadum
maþmum mislicum,   þæt hine mid nille,
100 ne mæg þære sawle   þe biþ synna ful
gold to geoce   for Godes egsan,
þonne he hit ær hydeð   þenden he her leofað.

99 *nille* (Sisam) : MS *wille*.

97–102] Probably the most disputed passage of the poem. Miss Kershaw refers to *Ynglinga saga*, chap. 8, where it is stated that according to Oðin's promise everyone shall bring to Valhalla such treasure as was placed on his funeral pyre and also what he had himself hidden in the ground during his lifetime. But, as Miss Daunt (*MLR* xi. 337) and Dr Sisam (*RES* xxi. 316) have shown, it is improbable that there is any reference to pagan custom here. Dr Sisam points out the parallels to Psalm 48 (West Saxon version). Still closer parallels are to be found in the OE homilies which in other passages, too, bear a close resemblance to the second part of *The Seafarer* (see Introd. p. 23 f.). But the poet seems to have combined two ideas which in the homilies are expressed separately: (i) that no man however nearly related to him can help the sinful one from the Judgement to come (cf. *Per se broþer þam oþrum ne mæg gehelpan, ne se fæder þam suna, ne þa neahmagas ne þa madm-ge-streon. Ne þysse worulde æhta ænigne man þer gescyldan ne mæg oþrum. Ac Drihten gyldeþ anra gehwylcum men æfter his sylfes gewyrhtum*; see Max Förster, *Festschrift für Lorenz Morsbach*, 134); and (ii) that wealth lavished on a man's grave is of no avail beyond the grave (cf. *ðeah þe ða mihtegestan and þa ricestan hatan him reste (byrgene) gewyrcan of marmanstane and mid goldfrætwum . . . and mid goldleafum gestrewed ymbutan, hwæðere se bitera deað þæt todæleð eal*; see Napier, 265 (148). We may take the general sense of the passage therefore to be that wealth, whether expended on his grave by his brother, or hoarded in his lifetime, cannot help the sinful man at the Final Judgement. The precise interpretation, however, is more difficult. Some take *deadum* (98) as sg., referring to the dead brother, and the object of *byrgan* to be the clause *þæt hine mid wille* (MS) in 99b ('Though brother will strew with gold the grave for his brother born, bury with the dead one in [the form of] various treasures that which he wishes [to go] with him, gold cannot help etc.'). As Dr Sisam points out, however, *byrgan* was restricted in early use to the burial of bodies. Moreover, if we take *þæt hine mid wille* (MS) as a noun clause, the sentence becomes awkward syntactically and logically in its blending of two separate ideas (though brother will strew the grave with gold . . . gold cannot help him when he hoarded it before). Dr Sisam's suggestion that 99[b] is the principal clause, requiring the insertion of a neg. seems the best solution: 'Though brother will strew with gold the grave for his brother born, bury [him] beside the dead with various treasures, that

45

Micel biþ se Meotudes egsa,   for þon hi seo molde
    oncyrreð;
se gestaþelade   stiþe grundas,
105 eorþan sceatas   ond uprodor.
Dol biþ se þe him his Dryhten ne ondrædeþ: cymeð
    him se deað unþinged.
Eadig欠 bið se þe eaþmod leofaþ;   cymeð him seo ar
    of heofonum.
Meotod him þæt mod gestaþelað,   for þon he in his
    meahte gelyfeð.
Stieran   mon sceal strongum mode,   ond þæt on
    staþelum healdan,
110 ond gewis werum,   wisum clæne.

109 *mon* (Thorpe): MS *mod*.

(i.e the gold) will not go with him; nor can gold be a help to the soul that
is full of sin in the presence of the terrible power of God, when he hoards it
beforehand while he is still alive on earth.' This use of *willan* would be unnatural syntax at an early date, but in later OE *willan* could be used to express the future tense, with no notion of volition, especially with reference to
habitual action or to what may be expected in a given condition.

golde stregan: cf. *mid goldleafum gestrewed ymbutan* in the homiletic passage
quoted above (Napier 263). This seems to suggest that the *golde* and the
maþmum mislicum refer to grave ornaments rather than to the heathen custom
of burying treasure with the dead. And the expression *græf stregan* (*streowan*)
may itself derive from a metaphorical use of the expression 'strew' or spread
a bed (Latin *lectum sternere*), cf. *morþorbed stred*, *Beow.* 2436.

for Godes egsan is sometimes rendered 'instead of the fear of God'; but in
other passages where this or a similar phrase occurs it appears to mean
'in the presence of (or because of) the terrible power of God'; cf. *Andreas*
457, *Gen.* 2592 etc. *Egsa* often denotes the power that inspires fear, as in
Judith 252, *Beow.* 3154, etc., and in the compounds *gledegesa*, *wæteregesa*,
etc.

103] 'Great is the terrible power of God, before which the earth will turn
aside.' Cf. *Apocalypsis* xx. 11: *a cujus conspectu fugit terra*. *hi* is acc. fem. reflex.

106] This same line occurs almost word for word in the Exeter Gnomic
Verses, 35: *Dol bið se þe his Dryhten nat, to þæs oft cymeð deað unþinged*.

109] *mon* (*mod* MS): the emendation, which has been generally adopted,
was suggested by line 50 of the Exeter Gnomic Verses: *Styran sceal mon
strongum mode*.

110] *ond gewis werum*: 'and [he must be] true to his pledges' (N. Kershaw). Mackie translates: 'and constant towards men'.

46

Scyle monna gehwylc   mid gemete healdan
†wiþ leofne ond wið laþne   * * * bealo.
† Þeah þe he ne wille   fyres fulne
oþþe on bæle   forbærnedne
115 his geworhtne wine,   Wyrd biþ swiþre,
Meotud meahtigra,   þonne ænges monnes gehygd.

113 *ne*: MS hine.
115 *swiþre* (Grein): MS swire.

___

111–12] Holthausen supplies *lufan* after *leofne* in 112: 'Let every man keep
moderation in love towards friend and enmity towards foe' (*Anglia Beibl*
xix. 248). But *bealo* in its active aspect implies wickedness or malice, which
would hardly be advocated even in moderation. Kemp Malone interprets
the lines as meaning that it is every man's duty to restrain his evil impulses
against friend and foe alike, and refers to BT Suppl A (xiv) for this meaning
of *healdan*. He inserts *gelice* after *laþne* to improve the metre (*Medium Ævum*
vi. 214 f). But since line 112 is defective and there is no clear connexion of
thought with what follows, it seems better to assume a lacuna.

113–15ª] These lines are defective metrically and the sense is obscure.
Holthausen attempts to restore the alliteration of 113 by altering the word-
order to *þeah þe he hine* (MS) *fyres fulne wille*, and inserts *seon* after *bæle* in 114
(*Anglia Beibl* xix. 248). Klaeber inserts *don*, and translates: 'Though he cause
him to be wrapped in fire and burnt on the funeral pyre, the friend he has
made'; and he adds that the general implication of the passage is 'that one's
love should be kept loyally beyond the friend's death' (*ESt* lxvii. 341).
Kemp Malone (*loc. cit.*) suggests that the meaning is: 'if one makes a friend,
and that friend prove false, so false that one would like to give him pagan
rather than Christian burial (in other words, damn him eternally), even
then, says the poet, one must do him no wrong'. Neither interpretation
seems very convincing, and it is more in keeping with the theme of the poem
to take the reference to fire to mean the fire of Hell. The phrase 'filled with
fire' is used in *Christ* 1562 of the damned in Hell, and *bæl* may refer to any
conflagration. The construction *þeah þe he wille* echoes line 97, and if we
assume a neg. the idea expressed repeats in a different form the idea expressed in 97–9 – that, though he may wish to save his near ones from the
Doom to come, he cannot. With the emendation of *hine* to *ne* in 113 (which
also eliminates the awkward anticipation of *his geworhtne wine* in 115) lines
113–16 may be translated: 'Though he may not wish the friend he has made
to be filled with fire or consumed in the conflagration, Doom is more powerful, God mightier, than any man's conception.' *Wyrd* is often equated in
Christian poetry and homily with the working of God's will, especially with
reference to the Doom to come (cf. *Blickling Homilies* 109, line 32). The
alliteration of 113 may be restored, if necessary, either by transposition of

Uton we hycgan   hwær we ham agen,
ond þonne geþencan   hu we þider cumen;
ond we þonne eac tilien   þæt we to moten
120 in þa ecan   eadignesse
þær is lif gelong   in lufan Dryhtnes,
hyht in heofonum.   Þæs sy þam Halgan þonc
þæt he usic geweorþade,   wuldres Ealdor
ece Dryhten,   in ealle tid.

                              Amen.

---

117 *hwær we* (Thorpe): MS hwær se.

---

the words, as suggested by Holthausen, or by emendation of *fyres* to *wylm-fyres*. The passage is abrupt and inconsequential as it stands and may have been misplaced by interpolation: see Introduction, p. 11. For the expression *geworhtne wine* cf. *Proverbs of Alfred* (Skeat's edition 129): *bute he him of fremde freond iwurche.*

117] A frequent homiletic formula.

119–20] *þæt we to moten*: *to* is adverbial, belonging to an unexpressed verb of motion. It anticipates and strengthens the force of *in* 'into' in the next line.

Select Bibliography

I. BIBLIOGRAPHICAL LISTS

For a comprehensive bibliography on Old English literature to 1972 see S.B. Greenfield and F.C. Robinson, *A Bibliography of Publications on Old English Literature to the End of 1972* (Toronto, 1980). For subsequent bibliography see *Old English Newsletter* or *Anglo-Saxon England* annually. The following are bibliographies on the Old English elegies and the Exeter Book. See also the bibliographies to the editions listed in Section 4.

1971 Knapp, W.B., 'Bibliography of the Criticism on the Old English Elegies', *Comitatus* 2, 71–90.

1983 Green, M., 'Elegy Scholarship 1973–82: a Select Bibliography' in *The Old English Elegies*, ed. M. Green, (Rutherford, Madison and Teaneck; London and Toronto), pp. 234–40.

1992 Conde Silvestre, J.C., '*The Wanderer* and *The Seafarer*: a Bibliography 1971–1991', *SELIM: Journal of the Spanish Society for Medieval English Language and Literature* 2, 170–86.

1992 Muir, B., *The Exeter Book: a Bibliography* (Exeter).

II. FACSIMILE

1993 Chambers, R.W., M. Förster and R. Flower, *The Exeter Book of Old English Poetry* (London).

III. THE MANUSCRIPT

1831–2 Chambers, R., *BL Add. MS 9067: a Transcript of the 'Exeter Book'*, London, British Library, collated with the manuscript by Frederick Madden in 1832.

1912 Chambers, R.W., 'The British Museum Transcript of The Exeter Book (Add. MS 9607)', *Anglia* 35, 393–400.

1933 Ker, N.R., 'Review of *The Exeter Book of Old English Poetry*', *Medium Ævum* 2, 224–31.

1934 Sisam, K., 'Review of *The Exeter Book of Old English Poetry*', *Review of English Studies* 10, 338–42.

1953 Sisam, K., 'The Exeter Book' in *Studies in the History of Old English Literature* (Oxford), pp. 97–108.

1953 Sisam, K., 'The Arrangement of the Exeter Book' in *Studies in the History of Old English Literature* (Oxford), pp. 291–2.

1957 Ker, N., *Catalogue of Manuscripts Containing Anglo-Saxon* (Oxford), no. 116.

1962 Blake, N., 'The Scribe of the Exeter Book', *Neophilologus* 46, 316–19.

1972 Dexter, K.M., 'The Exeter Book' in *Leofric of Exeter: Essays in Commemoration of the Foundation of Exeter Cathedral Library in A.D. 1072*, ed. F. Barlow et al. (Exeter), pp. 17–31.

1978 Drage, E.M., 'Bishop Leofric and the Exeter Cathedral Chapter (1050–1072): A Re-Assessment of the Manuscript Evidence' (unpublished DPhil dissertation, Oxford University).

1978 Pope, J.C., 'Paleography and Poetry: Some Solved and Unsolved Problems of the Exeter Book' in *Medieval Scribes, Manuscripts and Libraries: Essays Presented to N.R. Ker*, ed. M.B. Parkes and A.G. Watson (London), pp. 25–65.

1981 Gneuss, H., 'A Preliminary List of Manuscripts Written or Owned in England up to 1100', *Anglo-Saxon England* 9, 1–60, no. 257.

1986 Connor, P.W., 'The Structure of the Exeter Book Codex (Cathedral Library, MS. 3501)', *Scriptorium* 40, 233–42.

1986 Hill, J., 'The Exeter Book and Lambeth Palace Library MS. 149: A Reconsideration', *American Notes and Queries* 24, 112–16.

1989 Muir, B., 'A Preliminary Report on a New Edition of the Exeter Book', *Scriptorium* 43 (1989), 273–88.

1990 O'Brien O'Keeffe, K., *Visible Song: Transitional Literacy in Old English Verse*, Cambridge Studies in Anglo-Saxon England 4 (Cambridge), pp. 155–64 and 188–9.

1993 Connor, P.W., *Anglo-Saxon Exeter: A Tenth-Century Cultural History* (Woodbridge).

See also the editions of the text.

IV. EDITIONS

1842 Thorpe, B., *Codex Exoniensis: A Collection of Anglo-Saxon Poetry from a Manuscript in the Library of the Dean and Chapter of Exeter, with an English Translation, Notes and Indexes* (London) [with translation].

SELECT BIBLIOGRAPHY

1850 Ettmüller, L., *Engla and Seaxna Scopas and Boceras* (Quedlinburg and Berlin) [with translation].

1857 Grein, C.W.M., *Bibliothek der angelsächsischen Poesie I* (Göttingen); revised by R.P. Wülker (Kassel, 1883).

1882 Wülker, R.P., *Kleinere angelsächsische Dichtungen II* (Halle).

1888 Kluge, F., *Angelsächsisches Lesebuch* (Halle); fourth edition 1915.

1894 Sweet, H., *An Anglo-Saxon Reader*, seventh edition [first to include *Seafarer*] (Oxford); fifteenth edition revised by D. Whitelock as *Sweet's Anglo-Saxon Reader in Prose and Verse* (1967) [lines 1–108].

1915 Sieper, E., *Die altenglische Elegie* (Strassburg) [with German translation].

1919 Schücking, L.L., *Kleines angelsächsisches Dichterbuch* (Cöthen); repr. Leipzig, 1933.

1920 Imelmann, R., *Forschungen zur altenglischen Poesie* (Berlin) [lines 1–64a, with German translation].

1922 Kershaw, N., *Anglo-Saxon and Norse Poems* (Cambridge) [with translation].

1922 Sedgefield, W.J., *An Anglo-Saxon Verse Book* (Manchester) [lines 1–102]; re-issued in 1926 in *The Anglo-Saxon Book of Verse and Prose*.

1926 Wyatt, A.J., *The Threshold of Anglo-Saxon* (Cambridge) [lines 1–22 only]

1931 Craigie, W.A., *Specimens of Anglo-Saxon Poetry: III. Germanic Legend and Anglo-Saxon History and Life* (Edinburgh).

1934 Mackie, W.S., *The Exeter Book*, Part II, EETS O.S. 194 (London) [with translation].

1935 Anderson, M., and Williams, B.C., *An Old English Handbook* (Boston) [lines 1–108].

1936 Krapp, G.P., and Dobbie, E.V.K, *The Exeter Book* (London and New York).

1948 Ardern, P.S., *First Readings in Old English* (Wellington, N.Z.); revised edition 1951 [lines 1–64].

1966 Fowler, R., *Old English Prose and Verse: An Annotated Selection with Introductions and Notes* (London).

1966 Pope, J., ed., *Seven Old English Poems* (New York, 1966; 2nd ed. New York and London, 1981).

1970 Hamer, R., *A Choice of Anglo-Saxon Verse* (London) [with translation].

1972 Breuer, R., and R. Schwörling, ed., *Altenglische Lyrik, Englisch und deutsch* (Stuttgart).

1982 Mitchell, B., and Robinson, F.C., *A Guide to Old English* (Oxford, 1982; 5th ed., 1992).

1987 Butler, R.M., '*The Seafarer* 1–66a: An Approach to an Edition' (unpublished PhD dissertation, Duke University).

1991 Rodrigues, L.J., ed. and trans., *Seven Anglo-Saxon Elegies from the Exeter Book* (Felinfach).

1992 Klinck, A.L., *The Old English Elegies: a Critical Edition and Genre Study* (Montreal, Kingston, London and Buffalo).

1994 Muir, B.J., *The Exeter Anthology of Old English Poetry: An Edition of Exeter Dean and Chapter MS 3501*, 2 vols (Exeter).

V. REVIEWS OF GORDON'S EDITION

1961 Cross, J.E., *Journal of English and Germanic Philology* 60, 545–9.

1961 Elliott, R.W.V., *Modern Language Review* 56, 629.

1962 Stanley, E.G., *Medium Ævum* 31, 54–60.

1963 Ostheeren, K., *Anglia* 81, 465–9.

VI. TRANSLATIONS

See also the editions listed in Section IV.

1859 Grein, C.M.W., *Dichtungen der Angelsachsen* II (Göttingen).

1902 Cook, A.S., and Tinker, C.B., *Select Translations from Old English Poetry* (Boston); second edition 1926.

1926 Pound, E., 'The Seafarer from the Anglo-Saxon', *Personae* (New York), pp. 64–6; also in *The Collected Early Poems of Ezra Pound*, ed. M.J. King (London, 1977), pp. 188–90.

1926 Gordon, R.K., *Anglo-Saxon Poetry* (London and Toronto); revised edition 1954.

1934 Bone, G., 'The Seafarer', *Medium Ævum* 3, 1–6.

1936 Kennedy, C.W., *Old English Elegies* (Princeton).

1941 Malone, K., *Ten Old English Poems, Put into Modern Alliterative Verse* (Baltimore).

1954 Morgan, E., 'The Seafarer', *The European* [London] no. 14 (April), 51–3; repr. in *Medieval Age*, ed. A. Flores (New York, 1963).

1955 Whitelock, D., *English Historical Documents I, c. 500–1042* (London); second edition 1979.

1966 Alexander, M., *The Earliest English Poems* (London).

SELECT BIBLIOGRAPHY

1967 Hieatt, C.B., *'Beowulf' and Other Old English Poems* (Toronto); revised edition 1983.

1975 Austin, L.L., '*The Seafarer*: A Translation', *Old English Newsletter* 8.2, no page numbers.

1980 Wain, J., *The Seafarer* (Warwick).

1982 Bradley, S.A.J., *Anglo-Saxon Poetry. An Anthology of Old English Poems in Prose Translation* (London).

1986 Oldknow, A., 'Two Translations from Old English', *North Dakota Quarterly* 54.4, 18–24.

1990 Leavitt, N., and Young, K., *'The Seafarer', from the Anglo-Saxon Exeter Book, Translation by Karl Young* (Bangor, ME).

VII. TECHNICAL AND TEXTUAL STUDIES

1903 Strunk, W., Jr, 'Notes on the Shorter Old English Poems', *Modern Language Notes* 18, 72–3.

1907 Swaen, A.E.H., 'Some Old English Bird Names', *Archiv für das Studium der neueren Sprachen und Literaturen* 118, 387–9.

1908 Holthausen, F., 'Zur altenglischen Literatur VII', *Beiblatt zur Anglia* 19, 248–9.

1912–13 Sisam, K., 'To *Seafarer*, lines 72ff', *Englische Studien* 46, 336.

1916 Daunt, M., '*The Seafarer*, lines 97–102', *Modern Language Review* 11, 337–8.

1918 Daunt, M., 'Some Difficulties of *The Seafarer* reconsidered', *Modern Language Review* 13, 474–9.

1918 Kock, E.A., 'Jubilee Jaunts and Jottings', *Lunds Universitets Årsskrift*, n.s. 1, 14, no. 26, 1–82, at 75–7.

1920 Holthausen, F., 'Zu altenglischen Dichtungen, 2. *Der Seefahrer*', *Beiblatt zur Anglia* 31, 25–32.

1921 Holthausen, F., 'Review of Schücking, *Kleines angelsächsisches Dichterbuch*', *Beiblatt zur Anglia* 32, 80–3.

1922 Holthausen, F., 'Studien zu altenglischen Dichtungen, III', *Anglia* 46, 55–62.

1923–4 Craigie, W.A., 'Interpolations and Omissions in Anglo-Saxon Poetic Texts', *Philologica* 2, 5–19.

1924 Klaeber, F., 'Review of Sedgefield, *Anglo-Saxon Verse Book*', *Journal of English and Germanic Philology* 23, 121–4.

1927 Klaeber, F., 'Weitere Randglossen zu Texterklärungen', *Beiblatt zur Anglia* 38, 354–60.

1932–33 Klaeber, F., 'Three Textual Notes: 2. *Seafarer* 111–115', *Englische Studien* 67, 341–2.

1935 Holthausen, F., 'Review of Mackie, *Exeter Book, II*', *Beiblatt zur Anglia* 46, 5–10.

1937 Malone, K., 'On *Seafarer* 111–116', *Medium Ævum* 6, 214–15.

1945 Sisam, K., '*Seafarer* lines 97–102', *Review of English Studies* 21, 316–17.

1954 Goldsmith, M.E., '*The Seafarer* and the Birds', *Review of English Studies* n.s. 5, 225–35.

1960 Bolton, W.F., 'Connectives in *The Seafarer* and *The Dream of the Rood*', *Modern Philology* 57, 260–2.

1962 Blake, N.F., '*The Seafarer*, Lines 48–49', *Notes and Queries* 207, 163–4.

1962 Rigby, M., '"The Seafarer", "Beowulf", l. 769 and a Germanic Conceit', *Notes and Queries* 207, 246.

1962 Sisam, K., 'Old English *Stefn, Stefna,* "Stem"', *Review of English Studies* 13, 282–3.

1965 Pheifer, J.D., '*The Seafarer* 53–55', *Review of English Studies* 16, 282–4.

1967 Isaacs, N.D., '*The Seafarer* 109–115a', *English Studies* 48, 416–19.

1968 Mitchell, B., 'More Musings on Old English Syntax', *Neuphilologische Mitteilungen* 69, 53–63.

1968 Whittier, P.G., 'Spring in *The Seafarer* 48–50', *Notes and Queries* 213, 407–9.

1968–9 Cherniss, M.D., 'The Meaning of *The Seafarer*, Lines 97–102', *Modern Philology* 66, 146–9.

1971 Diekstra, F.N.M., '*The Seafarer* 58–66a: The Flight of the Exiled Soul to its Fatherland', *Neophilologus* 55, 433–46.

1973 Schubel, F., 'Der angelsächsische "klagende" Kuckuck', *Festschrift Prof. Dr. Herbert Koziol zum siebzigsten Geburtstag*, ed. G. Bauer, F.K. Stanzel and F. Zaic, Wiener Beiträge zur englischen Philologie 75 (Vienna and Stuttgart), 280–96.

1974 Green, B.K., 'The Seafarer's Joy: the Interpretation of lines 58a–64a', *University of Cape Town Studies in English* 5, 21–33.

1974 Kirby, 'Old English "*Ferð*"', *Notes and Queries* 219, 443.

1975 Howlett, D.R., 'The Structures of *The Wanderer* and *The Seafarer*', *Studia Neophilologica* 47, 313–17.

1976 Moore, B., '*The Seafarer* ll. 1–8a', *Explicator* 35.1, 11–12.

1977 Hill, J.M., '"þis deade lif": a Note on *The Seafarer*, Lines 64–66', *English Language Notes* 15, 95–7.

1977 Hultin, N., 'The External Soul in *The Seafarer* and *The Wanderer*', *Folklore* 88, 39–45.

1981 Cornell, M., 'Varieties of Repetition in Old English Poetry, Especially in *The Wanderer* and *The Seafarer*', *Neophilologus* 65, 292–307.

1982 Orton, P.R., '*The Seafarer* 58–64a', *Neophilologus* 66, 450–9.

1982 Orton, P.R., '*The Seafarer* 6b–10a and 18–22', *Neuphilologische Mitteilungen* 83, 255–9.

1983 Richardson, J., 'On *The Seafarer*, Line 34b', *Modern Philology* 81, 168–9.

1984 Stanley, E.G., 'Unideal Principles of Editing Old English Verse', *Proceedings of the British Academy* 70 (1984), 231–73, at 251–52.

1985 Mitchell, B., *Old English Syntax*, 2 vols (Oxford).

1985 Mitchell, B., 'The Syntax of *The Seafarer*, lines 50–52', *Review of English Studies* 36, 535–7.

1989 Vickrey, J.F., '*The Seafarer* 12–17, 25–30, 55–70: *Dives* and the Fictive Speaker', *Studia Neophilologica* 61, 145–56.

1990 Blockley, M., '*Seafarer* 82a: the Past as Perfect', *Notes and Queries* 235, 2–3.

1992 Ambrosini, R., 'On *The Wanderer* and *The Seafarer* Once Again, but from a Numerological Point of View', *Perspectives on Indo-European Language, Culture and Religion* (McLean, VA), II, 295–314.

1992 Hamer, R., '*The Seafarer*, Line 99b', *Notes and Queries* 237, 13–15.

1992 Vickrey, J.F., '*The Seafarer* 111–15: *Dives* and the Ultimate Futility', *Papers on Language and Literature* 28, 227–41.

1995 Vickrey, J.F., '*The Seafarer* 97–102: *Dives* and the Burial of Treasure', *Journal of English and Germanic Philology* 94, 19–30.

VIII. LITERARY STUDIES

1869 Rieger, M., 'Der *Seefahrer* als Dialog hergestellt', *Zeitschrift für deutsche Philologie* 1, 334–9.

1883 Kluge, F., 'Zu altenglischen Dichtungen. 1. Der *Seefahrer*', *Englische Studien* 6, 322–7.

1885 Kluge, F., 'Zu altenglischen Dichtungen. 2. Nochmals der *Seefahrer*', *Englische Studien* 8, 472–4.

1886 Hönncher, E., 'Zur Dialogeinteilung im *Seefahrer* (A) und zur zweiten homiletischen Partie (B) dieses Gedichtes', *Anglia* 9, 435–46.

1894 Ferrell, C.C., 'Old Germanic Life in the Anglo-Saxon *Wanderer* and *Seafarer*', *Modern Language Notes* 9, 201–4.

1902 Boer, R.C., '*Wanderer* und *Seefahrer*', *Zeitschrift für deutsche Philologie* 35, 1–28.

1902 Heusler, A., 'Der Dialog in der altgermanischen erzählenden Dichtung', *Zeitschrift für deutsches Altertum und deutsche Literatur* 46, 189–284.

1902 Lawrence, W.W., '*The Wanderer* and *The Seafarer*', *Journal of English and Germanic Philology* 4, 460–80.

1908 Imelmann, R., '*Wanderer*' und '*Seefahrer*' in Rahmen der altenglischen Odoaker-dichtung (Berlin).

1909 Ehrismann, G., 'Religionsgeschichtliche Beiträge zum germanischen Frühcristentum. II. Das Gedicht vom Seefahrer', *Beiträge zur Geschichte der deutschen Sprache und Literatur* 35, 213–18.

1917 Schücking, L.L., 'Die altenglische Elegie', *Englische Studien* 51, 97–115 [review of Sieper's edition].

1923 Heusler, A., *Die altgermanische Dichtung* (Wildpark-Potsdam).

1932 Idelmann, T., *Das Gefühl in den altenglischen Elegien* (Bochum).

1935 Wardale, E.E., *Chapters on Old English Literature* (London).

1936 Schücking, L.L., 'Heroische Ironie im angelsächsischen Seefahrer', in *Englische Kultur in sprachwissenschaftlicher Deutung: Festschrift für M. Deutschbein* (Leipzig), pp. 72–4.

1937–8 Anderson, O.S., '*The Seafarer*: an Interpretation', *K. Humanistiska Vetenkapssamfundets i Lund Årsberättelse* I (Lund).

1938 Schücking, L.L., 'Review of Anderson's "*The Seafarer*: an Interpretation"', *Beiblatt zur Anglia* 49, 301–3.

1938–9 Rosteutscher, J.H.W., 'Germanischer Schicksalsglaube und angelsächsische Elegiendichtung', *Englische Studien* 73, 1–31.

1941–2 Liljegren, S.B., 'Some Notes on the Old English Poem, *The Seafarer*', *Studia Neophilologica* 14, 145–59.

1942 Timmer, B.J., 'The Elegaic Mood in Old English Poetry', *English Studies* 24, 33–44.

1943 Kennedy, C.W., *The Earliest English Poetry* (London).

1944 Timmer, B.J., 'Heathen and Christian Elements in Old English Poetry', *Neophilologus* 29, 180–5.

1948 Grubl, E.D., *Studien zu den angelsächsischen Elegien* (Marburg).

1950 Whitelock, D., 'The Interpretation of *The Seafarer*', in *The Early Cultures of North-West Europe (H.M. Chadwick Memorial Studies)* (Cambridge), pp. 259–72; reprinted in *Essential Articles for the Study of Old English Poetry*, ed. J.B. Bessinger and S.J. Kahrl

SELECT BIBLIOGRAPHY

(Hamden, 1968), pp. 442–57, and in *Old English Literature: Twenty-Two Analytical Essays*, ed. M. Stevens and J. Mandel (Lincoln, Nebraska, 1968), pp. 198–211.

1954 Gordon, I.L., 'Traditional Themes in *The Wanderer* and *The Seafarer*', *Review of English Studies* n.s. 5, 1–13.

1954 Greenfield, S.B., 'Attitudes and Values in *The Seafarer*', *Studies in Philology* 51, 15–20; reprinted in his *Hero and Exile: The Art of Old English Poetry* (London and Ronceverte, 1989), pp. 155–60.

1955 Greenfield, S.B., 'The Formulaic Expression of the Theme of 'Exile' in Anglo-Saxon Poetry', *Speculum* 30 (1955), 200–6; reprinted in his *Hero and Exile* (1989), pp. 125–31.

1955 Stanley, E.G., 'Old English Poetic Diction and the Interpretation of *The Wanderer*, *The Seafarer* and *The Penitent's Prayer*', *Anglia* 73, 413–66; reprinted in *Essential Articles for the Study of Old English Poetry*, ed. J.B. Bessinger and S.J. Kahrl (Hamden, 1968), pp. 458–514, and in *A Collection of Papers with Emphasis on Old English Literature*, ed. E.G. Stanley (Toronto, 1987), pp. 234–80.

1956 Cross, J.E., 'Ubi Sunt Passages in Old English—Sources and Relationships', *Vetenskaps-Societeten i Lund Arsbok*, 25–44.

1957 and 1959 Smithers, G.V., 'The Meaning of *The Seafarer* and *The Wanderer*', *Medium Ævum* 26, 137–53; 28, 1–22, 99–104.

1959 Cross, J.E., 'On the Allegory in *The Seafarer*: Illustrative Notes', *Medium Ævum* 28, 104–6.

1960 Campbell, J.J., 'Oral Poetry in *The Seafarer*', *Speculum* 35, 87–96.

1960 Denny, N., 'Image and Symbol in *The Seafarer*', *Theoria* (Natal University College) 14, 29–35.

1960 O'Neil, W.A., 'Another Look at Oral Poetry in *The Seafarer*', *Speculum* 35, 596–600.

1960 Salmon, V., '*The Wanderer* and *The Seafarer*, and the Old English Conception of the Soul', *Modern Language Review* 55, 1–10.

1961 Bessinger, J.B., 'The Oral Text of Ezra Pound's "The Seafarer"', *Quarterly Journal of Speech* 47, 173–7.

1962 Cross, J.E., *Latin Themes in Old English Poetry, with an excursus on the Middle English 'Ubi Suont qui ante nos fuerount'*, (University of Lund: dissertation summary).

1963 Cross, J.E., 'Aspects of Microcosm and Macrocosm in Old English Literature', in *Studies in Old English Literature in Honor of Arthur G. Brodeur*, ed. S.B. Greenfield (New York), 1–22.

57

1964 Göller, K.H., 'Die angelsächsischen Elegien', *Germanische-Romanisch Monatsschrift* 45 (1964), 225–41.

1964 Prins, A.A., 'The *Wanderer* (and the *Seafarer*)', *Neophilologus* 48, 237–51.

1965 Pope, J.C., 'Dramatic Voices in *The Wanderer* and *The Seafarer*' in *Franciplegius: Medieval and Linguistic Studies in Honor of Francis Peabody Magoun, Jr*, ed. J.B. Bessinger and R.P. Creed (New York), pp. 164–93.

1965 Stevick, R.D., 'The Text and Composition of *The Seafarer*', *Publications of the Modern Language Association of America* 80, 332–6.

1966 Dietrich, G., 'Ursprünge des Elegischen in der altenglischen Literatur' in *Literatur-Kultur-Gesellschaft in England und Amerika: Aspekte und Forschungsbeiträge*, ed. G. Müller-Schwefe and K. Tuzinski (Frankfurt), pp. 3–27.

1966 Greenfield, S.B., 'The Old English Elegies' in *Continuations and Beginnings: Studies in Old English Literature*, ed. E.G. Stanley (London), pp. 142–75; reprinted in his *Hero and Exile* (1989), pp. 93–123.

1966 Henry, P.L., *The Early English and Celtic Lyric* (London).

1966 Isaacs, N.D., 'Image, Metaphor, Irony, Allusion, and Moral: The Shifting Perspective of *The Seafarer*', *Neuphilologische Mitteilungen* 67, 266–82.

1966 Pfeffer, A.S., '*The Seafarer*: Form and Theme', *Studies in Literature: Selected Papers by Graduate Students in English at the City University of New York* (New York), pp. 7–25.

1967 Irving, E.B., Jr, 'Image and Meaning in the Elegies' in *Old English Poetry: Fifteen Essays*, ed. R.P. Creed (Providence, RI), pp. 153–66.

1969 Campbell, T.P., 'The Treasure Motif in Four Old English Religious Elegies', *Revue de l'Université Laurentienne* 2.2, 45–58.

1969 Greenfield, S.B., '*Min, Sylf*, and "Dramatic Voices in *The Wanderer* and *The Seafarer*"', *Journal of English and Germanic Philology* 68, 212–20; reprinted in his *Hero and Exile* (1989), pp. 161–9.

1970 Whitbread, L., 'The Pattern of Misfortune in *Deor* and Other Old English Poems', *Neophilologus* 54, 167–83 (at 174–6).

1971 Bessai, F., 'The Two Worlds of the Seafarer', *Peregrinatio* 1, 1–8.

1971 Calder, D.G., 'Setting and Mode in *The Seafarer* and *The Wanderer*', *Neuphilologische Mitteilungen* 72, 264–75.

SELECT BIBLIOGRAPHY

1971 Gradon, P., *Form and Style in Early English Literature* (London), pp. 115–19.

1972 Empric, J.H., '*The Seafarer*: An Experience in Displacement', *Notre Dame English Journal* 7, 23–33.

1972 Greenfield, S.B., *A Critical History of Old English Literature* (New York).

1972 Greenfield, S.B., *The Interpretation of Old English Poems* (London and Boston).

1972 Lee, A.A., *The Guest-Hall of Eden* (New Haven and London).

1972 Shippey, T.A., *Old English Verse* (London), Chapter 3.

1972 Tripp, R.P., 'The Narrator as Revenant: a Reconsideration of Three Old English Elegies', *Papers on Language and Literature* 8, 339–61.

1973 Bosse, R.B., 'Aural Aesthetic and the Unity of *The Seafarer*', *Papers on Language and Literature* 9, 3–14.

1973 Campbell, A.P., '*The Seafarer*: Wanderlust and Our Heavenly Home', *Revue de l'Université d'Ottawa* 43, 235–47.

1973 Malmberg, L., 'Poetic Originality in *The Wanderer* and *The Seafarer*', *Neuphilologische Mitteilungen* 74, 220–3.

1973 Serio, J.N., 'Thematic Unity in *The Seafarer*', *Gypsy Scholar* 1, 16–21.

1974 Davenport, W.A., 'The Modern Reader and the Old English *Seafarer*', *Papers on Language and Literature* 10, 227–40.

1974 Hume, K., 'The Concept of the Hall in Old English Poetry', *Anglo-Saxon England* 3, 63–74.

1974 Pope, J.C., 'Second Thoughts on the Interpretation of *The Seafarer*', *Anglo-Saxon England* 3, 75–86.

1975 Green, M., 'Man, Time and Apocalypse in *The Wanderer*, *The Seafarer*, and *Beowulf*', *Journal of English and Germanic Philology* 74, 502–18.

1975 Klein, W.F., 'Purpose and the "Poetics" of *The Wanderer* and *The Seafarer*', in *Anglo-Saxon Poetry: Essays in Appreciation*, ed. L.E. Nicholson and D.W. Frese (Notre Dame, Indiana), pp. 208–23.

1975 Woolf, R., '*The Wanderer*, *The Seafarer*, and the Genre of Planctus', in *Anglo-Saxon Poetry: Essays in Appreciation*, ed. L.E. Nicholson and D.W. Frese (Notre Dame), pp. 192–207.

1976 Adams, S.J., 'A Case for Pound's *Seafarer*', *Mosaic* 9.2, 127–46.

1976 Alexander, M., 'Ezra Pound's Seafarer', *Agenda* 13.4/14.1, 110–26.

1976 Mandel, J., '*The Seafarer*', *Neuphilologische Mitteilungen* 77, 538–51.

1977 Chaplin, S., 'Pound's "Seafarer": an Assessment of Value', *Unisa English Studies* 15.2, 42–5.

1977 Green, B.K., 'Spes viva: Structure and Meaning in *The Seafarer*', *An Old English Miscellany presented to W.S. Mackie*, ed. B.S. Lee (Cape Town, London and New York), pp. 28–45.

1977 Pearsall, D., *Old English and Middle English Poetry*, Routledge History of English Poetry 1 (London, Henley and Boston), pp. 51–55.

1978 Osborn, M., 'Venturing upon Deep Waters in *The Seafarer*', *Neuphilologische Mitteilungen* 79, 1–6.

1979 Arngart, O., '*The Seafarer*: a Postscript', *English Studies* 60, 249–53.

1979 Goldman, S.H., 'The Use of Christian Belief in Old English Poems of Exile', *Res Publica Litterarum* 2, 69–80.

1979 Horgan, A.D., 'The Structure of *The Seafarer*', *Review of English Studies* 30, 41–9.

1980 Shields, J.C., '*The Seafarer* as a *Meditatio*', *Studia Mystica* 3.1, 29–41.

1981 Greenfield, S.B., '*Sylf*, Seasons, Structure and Genre in *The Seafarer*', *Anglo-Saxon England* 9, 199–211; reprinted in his *Hero and Exile* (1989), pp. 171–83.

1982 Alexander, M., *Old English Literature* (London), pp. 112–24.

1982 Dahlberg, C., '*The Seafarer*: the Wier-Metaphor and Benedictine Silence', *Mediaevalia* 6 (1982 for 1980), 11–35.

1982 Fujisawa, M., 'An Interpretation of the Old English Poem, *The Seafarer*', *Studies in English and American Literature* (Japan Women's University) 17, 85–99.

1982 Harris, J., 'Elegy in Old English and Old Norse: a Problem in Literary History', in *The Vikings*, ed. R.T. Farrell (Chicester), pp. 157–64; reprinted in *The Old English Elegies: New Essays in Criticism and Research*, ed. M. Green (Rutherford, Madison and Teaneck, NJ; London and Toronto, 1983).

1982 Holton, F.S., 'Old English Sea Imagery and the Interpretation of *The Seafarer*', *Yearbook of English Studies* 12, 208–17.

1982 Robinson, F.C., '"The Might of the North": Pound's Anglo-Saxon Studies and *The Seafarer*', *Yale Review* 71, 199–224.

1982 Vickrey, J.F., 'Some Hypotheses concerning *The Seafarer*', *Archiv für das Studium der neueren Sprachen und Literaturen* 219, 57–77.

1983 Foley, J.M., 'Genre(s) in the Making: Diction, Audience and Text in the Old English *Seafarer*', *Poetics Today* 4, 683–706.

1983 Fujisawa, M., 'The Image of "Exile" in *The Wanderer* and *The Seafarer*', *Studies in English and American Literature* (Japan Women's University) 18, 123–33.

1983 Gribble, B., 'Form and Function in Old English Poetry', *Language and Style* 16, 456–67.

1983 Higley, S.L., 'Lamentable Relationships? Non-Sequitur in Old English and Middle Welsh Elegy', in *Connections between Old English and Medieval Celtic Literature*, ed. P.K. Ford and K.G. Borst, Old English Colloquium ser. 2 (Lanham, MD), pp. 45–66.

1983 Leslie, R.F., 'The Meaning and Structure of *The Seafarer*', in *The Old English Elegies: New Essays in Criticism and Research*, ed. M. Green (Rutherford, Madison and Teaneck, NJ; London and Toronto), pp. 96–122.

1983 Raffel, B., 'Translating Old English Elegies', in *The Old English Elegies*, ed. M. Green, pp. 31–45.

1984 Bately, J., 'Time and the Passing of Time in "The Wanderer" and related Old English Texts', *Essays and Studies* n.s. 37, 1–15.

1984 Klinck, A.L., 'The Old English Elegy as a Genre', *English Studies in Canada* 10, pp. 129–40.

1985 Godden, M.R., 'Anglo-Saxons on the Mind', in *Learning and Literature in Anglo-Saxon England*, ed. M. Lapidge and H. Gneuss (Cambridge), pp. 271–98.

1986 Greenfield, S.B., and D.G. Calder, *A New Critical History of Old English Literature* (New York and London), pp. 287–88.

1987 Earl, J.W., 'Transformation of Chaos: Immanence and Transcendence in *Beowulf* and Other Old English Poetry', *Ultimate Reality and Meaning* 10, 164–85.

1987 Mandel, J., *Alternative Readings in Old English Poetry*, American University Studies, ser. 4: English Language and Literature 43 (New York).

1987 McPherson, C., 'The Sea a Desert: Early English Spirituality and *The Seafarer*', *American Benedictine Review* 38, 115–26.

1987 Swanton, M., *English Literature before Chaucer* (London and New York), pp. 114–22.

1989 Jacobs, N., 'Syntactical Connection and Logical Disconnection: the Case of *The Seafarer*', *Medium Ævum* 58, 105–13.

1989 Williams, D., ' "The Seafarer" as an Evangelical Poem', *Lore and Language* 8.1, 19–30.

1990 Caie, G.D., 'The Exile Figure in Old English Poetry', *Europa og de Fremmede i Middelalderen*, ed. K.V. Jensen (Copenhagen, 1989), pp. 71–81.

1990 Cucina, C., *Sulla struttura del 'Seafarer': la tipologia del contrasto come strategia compositiva*, Studi e ricerche di linguistica e filologia 3 (Pavia).

1990 Hoople, S.C., '*Stefn*: the Transcendent Voice in *The Seafarer*', *In Geardagum* 11, 45–55.

1990 Morgan, G., 'Essential Loss: Christianity and Alienation in the Anglo-Saxon Elegies', *In Geardagum* 11, 15–33.

1990 Tristram, H.L.C., 'The Early Insular Elegies: *item alia*', in *Celtic Linguistics*, ed. M.J. Ball et al., Current Issues in Linguistic Theory 69 (Amsterdam and Philadelphia), 343–61.

1991 Bragg, L. *The Lyric Speakers of Old English Poetry* (Rutherford, NJ, London and Toronto).

1991 Fell, C., 'Perceptions of Transience', in *The Cambridge Companion to Old English Literature*, ed. M. Godden and M. Lapidge (Cambridge), pp. 172–89.

1991 McNichols, M.D., 'Survivals and (Re)newals: Pound's "The Seafarer"', *Paideuma* 20.1–2, 113–27.

1991 Orton, P., 'The Form and Structure of *The Seafarer*', *Studia Neophilologica* 63, 37–55.

1992 Donavin, G., 'A Preacher's Identity: Allusions to Jonah in *The Seafarer*', *Yearbook of English Studies* 22, 28–37.

1992 Foley, J.M., 'Oral Traditional Aesthetics and Old English Poetry', *Medialität und mittelalterliche insulare Literatur*, ed. H.L.C. Tristram (Tübingen), pp. 80–103.

1992 Magennis, H., 'Images of Laughter in Old English Poetry, with Particular Reference to the "hleahtor wera" of *The Seafarer*', *English Studies* 73, 193–204.

1992 Zymer, T., '*Wyrd* as the Determiner of Human Fate in Selected Passages from Old English Poetry', *Kwartalnik Neofilologiczny* 39, 103–24.

1993 Higley, S.L., *Between Languages: the Uncooperative Text in Early Welsh and Old English Nature Poetry* (University Park, PA).

1993 Larrington, C., *A Store of Common Sense: Gnomic Theme and Style in Old Icelandic and Old English Wisdom Poetry* (Oxford), especially pp. 192–7.

1994 Earl, J.W., *Thinking about Beowulf* (Stanford), pp. 56–61.

IX. SOURCES AND COMPARATIVE MATERIAL

This section of the bibliography inevitably overlaps with others, in particular with Section VIII, Literary Studies.

1874–80 *The Blickling Homilies*, ed. R. Morris, Early English Text Society, Original Series 58, 63 and 73 (London); reprinted as one volume, 1967.

1883 *Wulfstan: Sammlung der ihm zugeschriebenen Homilien*, ed. A. Napier (Berlin).

1889 *Defensor's Liber Scintillarum*, ed. E.W. Rhodes, Early English Text Society, Original Series 93 (London).

1913 Förster, M., 'Der Vercelli-Codex CXVII nebst Abdruck einiger altenglischer Homilien der Handschrift' in *Festschrift für Lorenz Morsbach*, ed. F. Holthausen and H. Spies (Halle), pp. 20–179.

1919 Brandl, A., 'Venantius Fortunatus und die angelsächsische Elegien *Wanderer* und *Ruine*', *Archiv für das Studium der neueren Sprachen und Literaturen* 139, 84.

1932 Chadwick, H.M. and N.K., *The Growth of Literature I* (Cambridge).

1932 Williams, I., 'The Poems of Llywarch Hen', *Proceedings of the British Academy* 18, 269–302.

1935 Jackson, K., *Studies in Early Celtic Nature Poetry* (Cambridge).

1944 Williams, I., *Lectures on Early Welsh Poetry* (Dublin).

1954 Bromwich, R., 'The Character of the Early Welsh Tradition' in *Studies in Early British History*, ed. H.M. Chadwick and others (Cambridge), pp. 83–136.

1964 Chadwick, N.K., 'The Celtic Background of Early Anglo-Saxon England' in *Celt and Saxon. Studies in the Early British Border*, ed. K. Jackson et al. (Cambridge), pp. 323–52.

1964 Pilch, H., 'The Elegaic Genre in Old English and Early Welsh Poetry', *Zeitschrift für celtische Philologie* 29, 209–24.

1969 Clemoes, P.A.M., '*Mens absentia cogitans* in *The Seafarer* and *The Wanderer*' in *Medieval Literature and Civilization: Studies in Memory of G.N. Garmonsway*, ed. D.A. Pearsall and R.A. Waldron (London), 62–77.

1975 Luiselli Fadda, A.M., 'L'influsso dell'Ecclesiastico e dei Proverbi sui versi 111–116 dell'elegia anglosassone *Seafarer*', *Vetera Christianorum* 12, 383–9.

1976 Calder, D.G., and Allen, M.J.B., *Sources and Analogues of Old English Poetry: The Major Latin Texts in Translation* (Cambridge), pp. 134–53.

1983 Calder, D.G., R.E. Bjork, P.K. Ford and D.F. Melia, *Sources and Analogues of Old English Poetry II: The Major Germanic and Celtic Texts in Translation* (Cambridge), pp. 23–69.

1988 Galloway, A., '1 Peter and *The Seafarer*', *English Language Notes* 25.4, 1–10.

1990 Jacobs, N., 'Celtic Saga and the Contexts of Old English Elegiac Poetry', *Études Celtiques* 26, 95–142.

1990 Rowland, J., *Early Welsh Saga Poetry* (Cambridge).

1991 Ireland, C., 'Some Analogues of the OE *Seafarer* from Hiberno-Latin Sources', *Neuphilologische Mitteilungen* 92, 1–14.

1992 *The Vercelli Homilies and Related Texts*, ed. D.G. Scragg, Early English Text Society, Original Series 300 (Oxford).

Glossary

In the Glossary words will be found under the forms in which they occur, except that nouns, pronouns and adjectives (excluding irregular comparatives and the like) will be found under the nom. sg. masc., and verbs normally under the infin., except *uton* and the different stems of the verb 'to be'. Preceding a line reference * indicates a restored or emended form, and n following a line number refers to the appropriate note.

The order of the letters is alphabetical; *æ* is treated as a separate letter after *a*; *þ* and *ð* after *t*.

For other commonly accepted abbreviations see the earlier volumes published in this series.

A

ā, *adv.* always, ever 42, 47

ac, *conj.* (usually following a neg. clause) but 47

ādl, *f. ō-stem*, sickness, disease 70

āgan, *pret. pres. v.* [OWE]; own, have; **āh,** *pres. 3 sg.* 27; **āgen,** *pres. subj. pl.* 117

āh, see **āgan**

ānfloga, *m. n-stem*, solitary flier 62 n.

ār, *f. ō-stem*, grace, mercy 107

atol, *adj.* hateful, terrible 6

āwa, *adv.* always 79

Æ

æfter, *adv.* AFTERwards: after death 77

æftercweðende, *pres. pt. as sb. pl.* those speaking (of a man) after (his death) 72

ælde, *m. i-stem pl.* men 77

ænig, *adj.* ANY; **ænges,** *gen.* 116

ǣr, *adv.* ERE; beforehand 102; *prep.* before, until 69 n.; *conj. w. subj.* before 74

æt, *prep. w. dat.* AT 7

æþeling, *m. a-stem*, prince, noble 93

65

B

bǣl, *n. a-stem,* conflagration 114 n.

be, *prep. w. dat.* BY; beside 98; by, near 8; about, concerning 1

bealosīþ, *m. a-stem,* wandering (or experience) fraught with pain or hardship 28

bearn, *n. a-stem,* [BAIRN]; child, son 93 (pl.); *ælda bearn,* children of men 77

bearo, *m. wa-stem,* wood, grove 48

bēatan, *v.* (*7b*), BEAT; **bēotan,** *p.t.pl.* 23

bēodan, *v.* (*2*), BODE; announce, forebode 54

bēon, *anom. v.* BE; **biþ,** *pres. 3 sg.* (expressing general condition) is (ever) 44, *72, 100, 103, etc; *cf.* **is, nearon**

beorn, *m. a-stem,* warrior, man 55

bēotan, see **bēatan**

betst, *adj. sup.* BEST 73 (as sb.)

bīdan, *v.* (*1*), remain 30

gebīdan, *v.* (*1*), experience; **gebiden,** *p.pt.* 4, 28 n.

bidrēosan, *v.* (*2*) *w. dat.* deprive; **bidroren,** *p.pt.* bereaved of 16

bidroren, see **bidrēosan**

bigeal, *see* **bigiellan**

bigeat, see **bigietan**

bigiellan, *v.* (*3*), [YELL]; scream round about; **bigeal,** *p.t.* 24 n.

bigietan, *v.* (*5*), [GET]; keep, occupy; **bigeat,** *p.t.* 6

bihōn, *v.* (*7*), HANG around (with); **bihongen,** *p.pt. w. instr.* 17

bihongen, see **bihōn**

bindan, *v.* (*3*), BIND; **bond,** *p.t.* gripped 32; **gebunden,** *p.pt.* 9

bisgo, *f. ō-stem,* toil, trouble 88

bitter, *adj.* BITTER, grievous 4, 55 n.

biþ, see **bēon**

blācian, *w.v.* (*2*), grow pale 91

blǣd, *m. a-stem,* glory, *79, 88

blōstma, *m. n-stem,* BLOSSOM 48

bond, see **bindan**

geboren, *p.pt. as sb.* born in the same family, brother 98

brēostcearo, *f. ō-stem,* [BREAST + CARE]; sorrow of heart 4

brēosthord, *n. a-stem,* [BREAST + HOARD]; (innermost) feelings of the heart 55

brimlād, *f. ō-stem,* sea-way, path of ocean 30

brōþor, *m. r-stem,* BROTHER 98

brūcan, *v.* (2), possess, enjoy 88

gebunden, see **bindan**

burh, *f. cons-stem,* [BOROUGH, BURG(H)]; dwelling of men 28 n; **byrig,** *pl.* 48

būtan, *conj.* (*after neg.*), BUT, except 18

byrgan, *w.v.* (1), BURY 98

byrig, see **burh**

C

cald, *n. a-stem,* (the) cold 8

cald, *adj.* COLD, chill 10; **caldast,** *sup.* 33

cāsere, *m. ja-stem,* [CAESAR]; emperor 82

cearo, *f. ō-stem,* CARE, sorrow 10 (*pl.*)

cearseld, *n. a-stem,* abode of care; region where sorrow is experienced 5 n.

cēol, *m. a-stem,* [KEEL *sb.*²]; ship 5

clǣne, *adj. ja-stem,* CLEAN, pure 110

clif, *n. a-stem,* CLIFF 8

clomm, *m. a-stem,* grip, fetter 10

cnossian, *w.v.* (2), dash, drive 8 n.

cnyssan, *w.v.* (1), beat against; (fig.) trouble, oppress 33 n.

corn, *n. a-stem,* CORN, grain 33

cuman, *v.* (4), COME; **cymeð,** *pres. 3 sg.* 61, 106 (*fut.*), 107

cunnian, *w.v.* (2), [CUN]; explore, venture upon 5, 35

cymeð, see **cuman**

cyning, *m. a-stem,* KING 82

D

dagas, see **dæg**

dǣd, *f. i-stem,* DEED 41, 76

dæg, *m. a-stem,* DAY; **dagas,** *pl.* 80

dēad, *adj.* DEAD, *fig.* 65 n.; *quasi sb.* (the) dead 98

dēað, *m. a-stem,* DEATH 106

dēofol, *m. and n. a-stem,* the DEVIL 76

dēor, *adj.* [DEAR, DERE, *adj.*² (*obs.*)]; bold, brave 41, 76

dol, *adj.* [DULL]; foolish 106

dōm, *m. a-stem* [DOOM]; glory, renown 85

dōn, *w.v. anom.* DO; **dyde,** *p.t.* in *dyde ic me to gomene,* took for (had as) my entertainment 20

gedōn, *w.v. anom.* bring (to a condition or state); *to hwon hine Dryhten gedon wille,* concerning what (fate) the Lord will assign him, 43 n.

drēam, *m. a-stem,* [DREAM, *sb.*²]; joy, bliss 65, 80, 86

67

drēogan, *v.* (*2*), [DREE]; suffer, endure 56

drēosan, *v.* (*2*), fall, decline; **gedroren,** *p.pt.* 86

gedroren, see **drēosan**

dryhten, *m. a-stem,* lord; *his dryhten,* his (earthly) lord 41 n.; *Dryhten,* the (heavenly) Lord 43, 65, 106, 121, 124

dryhtlīc, *adj.* lordly, magnificent 85 (*sup.*).

duguð, *f. i-* and *ō-stem,* company of noble warriors, chivalry 86; (heavenly) host 80

dyde, see **dōn**

E

ēac, *adv.* [EKE]; also, moreover 119

ēadig, *adj.* blessed 107

ēadignes, *f. jō-stem,* beatitude, bliss 120

ealdian, *w.v.* (*2*), grow OLD 89

ealdor, *n. a-stem,* life, age; *awa to ealdre,* for ever and ever 79

Ealdor, *m. a-stem,* Prince, Lord 123

eal(l), *adj.* ALL 50, 81, 86, 124

eard, *m. a-* and *u- stem,* country, native land, home 38 n.

earfoðhwīl, *f. ō-stem,* time of hardship 3

earmcearig, *adj.* wretched and sorrowful 14 n.

earn, *m. a-stem,* [ERNE]; eagle 24

ēaþmōd, *adj.* humble, submissive 107

ēce, *adj. ja-stem,* eternal 79, 120, 124; for ever 67

ecghete, *m. i-stem,* swordhatred; violence of war or feud 70

eft, *adv.* again, back again 61

egsa, *m. n-stem,* terror, awful power 101 n., 103

elles, *adv.* ELSE 46

elþēodig, *adj.* alien; (as sb.) one who sojourns as an alien, *peregrinus,* 38 n.

engel, *m. a-stem,* angel 78

eorl, *m. a-stem,* [EARL]; warrior, man 72

eorþe, *f. n-stem,* EARTH; ground 32, 93; the earth, the world 39, 61, 81, 89, 105

eorþwela, *m. n-stem,* EARTH-WEALTH; *pl.* worldly prosperity 67

ēþel, *m. a-stem,* native land, home; *hwæles eþel,* haunt of the whale, the sea 60

F

faran, *v.* (*6*), FARE; go; *him on fareð,* overtakes him 91 n.

fǣge, *adj. ja-stem,* [FEY]; doomed to die 71

fægrian, *w.v.* (*2*), [FAIR, *v.*]; make beautiful, adorn 48 n.

fægrost, *adv. sup.* most happily 13 n.

feallan, *v.* (*7*), FALL; **fēol,** *p.t.* 32

fēasceaftig, *adj.* wretched, desolate 26

fela, *noun indecl. w. gen.* many 5

gefēlan, *w.v.* (*1*), FEEL 95

fēol, see **feallan**

fēond, *m. nd-stem,* FIEND, enemy 75

feor, *adv.* FAR, far away 37, 52

feorg, feorh, *m. and n. a-stem,* life 71, 94

fēran, *w.v.*(*1*), go, journey 37

ferð, *m. and n. a-stem,* heart, spirit 26, 37 n.

fēt, see **fōt**

flǣschoma, *m. n-stem,* covering of flesh, body 94

flēag, see **flēogan**

flēogan, *v.* (*2*), FLY; **flēag,** *p.t.* 17

flōdwegas, *m.pl.* [FLOOD + WAYS]; paths of the ocean 52 n.

folde, *f. n-stem,* earth, land 13 n.; (this) earth 75

for, *prep. w. instr.* FOR, because of (*or* before, in the presence of), 101 n.; **for**

þon, *adv.* therefore 72; and so, in truth, 27; *correlative adv.* 33, 58; *conj.* because 39, 64, 108; before, or because of, which 103 n.

forbærnan, *w.v.* (*1*), BURN up, consume (in fire) 114

fore, *prep. w. dat.* FOR, in place of 21, 22

forgiefan, *v.* (*5*) GIVE up (to) 93

forst, *m. a-stem,* FROST 9

forswelgan, *v.* (*3*), SWALLOW, eat 95

fōt, *m. cons-stem,* FOOT; **fēt,** *pl.* FEET 9

frēfran, *w.v.* (*1*), comfort 26

gefremman, *w.v.* (*1*), accomplish, perform 84

fremu, *f.,* beneficial action, good conduct *75 n.

fromweard, *adj.* (lit. facing away), about to depart, or die 71

ful, *adj. w. gen.* FULL (of) 100, 113; *adv.* very 24

fundian, *w.v.* (*2*), be eager to go, set out eagerly 47

fūs, *adj.* eager, ready to go 50

fȳr, *n. a-stem* FIRE 113

G

ganet, *m. a-stem,* GANNET 20

gēac, *m. a-stem,* cuckoo 53

gēoc, *f. ō-stem,* help 101

69

geoguþ, *f. ō-stem,* YOUTH, youthfulness 40

gēomor, *adj.* melancholy 53

geond, *prep. w. acc.* [YOND, *prep.*]; throughout 90

giellan, *v.* (*3*), [YELL]; cry 62

gifo, *f. ō-stem,* gift 40

gīfre, *adj. ja-stem,* eager, full of fierce longing 62

gnornian, *w.v.* (*2*), mourn, lament 92

gōd, *adj.* GOOD, generous 40

God, *m. a-stem,* GOD 101

gold, *n. a-stem,* GOLD 97, 101

goldgiefa, *m. n-stem,* gold-giver, lord 83

gomelfeax, *adj.* hoary-haired 92

gomen, *n. a-stem,* [GAME]; entertainment 20

grǣdig, *adj.* GREEDY; full of eager longing 62

græf, *n. a-stem,* GRAVE 97

grund, *m. a-stem,* GROUND; *pl.* foundations, the earth 104

H

habban, *w.v.* (*3*), HAVE; **hæbbe,** *pres. 1 sg.* 4; **hafað,** *pres. 3 sg.* 47; **næbbe** (*w. neg.*) *pres. 3 sg. subj.* 42

hafað, see **habban**

hālig, *adj.* HOLY; *þam Halgan,* (to) Holy God 122

hām, *m. a-stem,* HOME 117

hāt, *adj.* HOT 11 n.; **hātra,** *compar.* warmer, more living and inspiring 64 n.

hæbbe, see **habban**

hægl, *m. a-stem,* HAIL 17, 32

hē, *pron. m.* HE 42, 74, 102 etc.; it 8; **hine,** *acc.* him 43, 77, 99 etc. **him,** *dat.* to (*or* for) him 41, 44, 91, 94; *refl.* 27, 106; *þe him,* to whom, 13; **hī,** *fem. acc. refl.* itself 103; **hit,** *n. acc.* it 102; **hī,** *pl.* they 84; **him,** *dat. pl.* them 23, *refl.* themselves 84

hēah, *adj.* HIGH; deep; *hean streamas,* deep (*or* towering) seas 34 n

healdan, *v.* (*7*), HOLD, possess 87; keep, control 109, 111

hearpe, *f. n-stem,* HARP 44

heofon, *m. a-stem,* HEAVEN 107, 122

heonan, *adv.* hence 37

heorte, *f. n-stem,* HEART 11, 34

hēr, *adv.* HERE, (in this world) 102

hergan, *w.v.* (*1*), praise, extol 77

hī, hine, him, hit, see **hē**

his, *poss. adj.* his 40, 41, 42 etc.

hleahtor, *m. a-stem,* LAUGHTER 21

hlēomǣg, *m. a-stem,* protecting kinsman 25

hlēoþor, *n. a-stem,* sound, cry 20

hlimman, *v. (3),* roar, resound 18

hnǣgan, *w.v. (1),* bring low, humble 88

hold, *adj.* friendly, gracious 41

holm, *m. a-stem,* [HOLM(E)[1]]; sea; *pl.* ocean 64 *(gen.)*

hond, *f. u-stem,* HAND 96

hreþer, *m. or n. a-stem,* heart 63

hreþerloca, *m. n-stem,* enclosure of the heart, the breast 58 (cf. *ferðloca, Wand.* 13)

hrīm, *m. a-stem,* RIME, frost 32

hrīmgicel, *m.* icicle 17

hringþegu, *f.,* receiving of rings (by a liegeman from his lord) 44

hrūse, *f. n-stem,* earth, ground 32

hū, *conj. adv.* HOW 2, 14, 29, 118

huilpe, *f. n-stem,* WHAUP, curlew 21 n.

hungor, *m. a-stem,* HUNGER 11 n.

gehwā, *pron. (prec. by partit. gen.),* each, every 72

hwæl, *m. a-stem,* WHALE 60

***hwælweg,** *m. a-stem,* [WHALE + WAY]; path of the whale, the sea 63 n.

hwǣr, *rel. adv.* WHERE 117

hwæt, *pron. n.* WHAT 56; **hwon,** *instr.* 43

hwæt, *adj.* vigorous, active 40

hweorfan, *v. (3),* turn, go, journey 58, 60

hwettan, *w.v. (1),* WHET, incite 63

hwīlum, *adv.* [WHILOM]; at times 19

hwon, see **hwæt,** *pron. n.*

hwōn, *adj. as sb.* little, few *(w. gen.)* 28

gehwylc, *pron.* each, every 36, 68, 90, 111

hycgan, *w.v. (3),* think, consider 117

hȳdan, *w.v. (1),* HIDE, hoard 102

gehygd, *f. and n. i-stem,* thought, conception 116

hyge, *m. i-stem,* thought 44; mind 96; heart, spirit 58

hyht, *m. i-stem,* joy, pleasure 45, bliss 122

gehȳran, *w.v. (1),* HEAR 18

I

ic, *pron.* I 1, 2, 14 etc.; **mec,** *acc.* me 6; **mē,** *dat.* 1 (see **sylf**), 61; to, or for, me 20 *(refl.),* 64

in, *prep. w. dat.* IN 5, 28, 40, 41, 108, 121, 122; on 30; *w. acc.* into, to 55, 120; *(of time)* during 124

indryhto, *f.* nobility 89

innan, *adv.* from within 11

is, *pres. 3 sg.* IS 86, 88, 121; **nis,** is not 39; *****nearon,** *pl.* are not 82

īscald, -ceald, *adj.* ICE-COLD 14, 19

īsigfeþera, *w. adj.* having icy feathers 24

iū, *adv.* formerly, of old 83

iūwine, *m. i-stem,* friend (or lord) of former days 92

L

gelāc, *n.* motion, play; tumult 35

lagu, *m. u-stem,* sea, water 47

gelagu, *n. pl.* a collection of water, expanse (of ocean) 64

lāst, *m. a-stem,* [LAST, *sb.*¹]; track, footprint; *wræccan lastum,* in the paths of exile 15

lāstword, *n. a-stem,* reputation left behind (after death), 73

lāþ, *adj.* [LOATH]; (*as sb.*) foe 112

lǣne, *adj. ja-stem,* transitory, brief 66

lecgan, *w.v.* (*1*), LAY, set 57 (see **wrǣclāstas**).

lēof, *adj.* [LIEF]; dear, beloved; (*as sb.*) friend 112

leofað, see **lifgan**

līf, *n. a-stem,* LIFE 27, 65, 79, 121

lifgan (**lifian**), *w.v.* (*3*), LIVE 78 (*subj.*); **leofað,** *pres. 3. sg.* 102, 107; **lifdon,** *p.t. pl.* 85; **lifgende,** *pres. pt. as sb.* the living 73

limpan, *v.* (*3*), happen; *impers. w. dat.* 13 n.

lof, *n. and m. a-stem,* praise 73; glory 78

lond, *n. a-stem,* LAND 66 n.

gelong, *adj.* [ALONG, *adj.*]; belonging to, dependent on; *þær is lif gelong,* where is the source of life 121

longung, *f. ō-stem,* LONGING; yearning, anxiety 47 n.

losian, *w.v.* (*2*), [LOSE]; be lost, fail 94

lufu, *f. ō-stem* (*with oblique cases often n-stem*), LOVE 121

lust, *m. a-stem,* longing, desire 36

gelȳfan, *w.v.* (*1*), believe 66; (*w. refl. dat.*) 27; trust (in) 108

lȳt, *indecl. as sb. used with adv. force,* little 27

M

magan, *w.v. pret. pres.* [MAY]; be able; **mæg,** *pres. 1 and 3 sg.* (*auxil.*) can (or will) 1 n.; be of avail 94, 100; **meahte,** *p.t.* could 26

māþm (māþum), *m. a-stem,* treasure, precious or valuable thing 99

mæg, see **magan**

mǣl, *n. a-stem,* [MEAL, *sb.*[2]]; time, occasion 36

mǣrþo, *f. ō-stem,* glorious deed 84 (*gen. pl.*)

mǣst, *superl. adj. as sb.* MOST; the greatest 84

mǣw, *m. i-stem,* MEW; seagull 22

mē, mec, see **ic**

meaht, *f. i-stem,* MIGHT, power 108

meahte, see **magan**

meahtig, *adj.* MIGHTY 116 (*compar.*)

medodrinc, *m. a-stem,* [MEAD + DRINK]; mead 22

Meotod, Meotud, *m. a-stem,* Ordainer of fate, God 103, 108, 116

mereflōd, *m. a-stem,* [MERE + FLOOD]; sea-tide, ocean 59

merewērig, *adj.* [MERE + WEARY]; *as sb.* one weary of (or through journeying on) the sea; **merewērges,** *gen. sg.* 12

gemet, *n.* measure; *mid gemete,* with moderation (or, meetly, in fitting fashion) 111

micel, *adj.* [MUCH]; great 103

mid, *prep. w. dat.* with; along

with 59; among 78; *w. instr.* with, by means of, 96, 111; *w. acc.* along with 99

middangeard, *m. a-stem,* [MIDDENERD]; (this) world 90

mīn, *poss. adj.* my 9, 58, 59

mislīc, *adj.* various, diverse 99

mōd, *n. a-stem,* [MOOD]; heart, spirit 12, 36, 50, 108; temper 109

mōdsefa, *m. n-stem,* spirit, heart 59

mōdwlonc, *adj.* proud of heart, spirited 39

molde, *f. n-stem,* [MOULD, *sb.*[1]]; (this) earth 103

mon, *m. cons-stem,* MAN 12, 39, 90 etc.

(ge)monian, *w.v.* (*2*), remind, urge 36, 50, 53

mōtan, *w.v. pret. pres.* may, be allowed 119 (*subj.*).

N

naca, *m. n-stem,* boat, ship 7

nāp, see **nīpan**

***nearon,** see **is**

næbbe, see **habban**

nǣnig, *adj.* (*used substantively w. gen. pl.*), none 25

ne, *neg. adv.* not 12, 18, 44, 55, 94, etc.; *conj.* nor 40, 41, 44, 45, 46, 82, 83, 96;

neither ... nor 95; *fused with verbal forms* 39, 42, 82

nearo, *adj. wa-stem*, NARROW, close; *fig.* anxious 7

nefne, *conj.* except, but 46

nihtscūa, *m. n-stem*, shade of NIGHT 31

nihtwaco, *f.* [NIGHT + WAKE, *sb.*[1]]; night-watch 7

niman, *v. (4)*, [NIM]; take, assume 48 n.

nīpan, *v. (1)*, grow dark; **nāp,** *p.t.* 31

nis, see **is**

nīþ, *m. a-stem*, hatred, malice 75

nō, *emphatic neg.* not at all, not 66

norþan, *adv.* from the NORTH 31

nū, *adv.* NOW 33, 58, 82, 90

O

of, *prep. w. dat.* [OF, OFF]; from 107

ofer, *prep. w. acc.*, (of motion) OVER, across 60, 64; beyond 58; (of extent) throughout 39

oft, *adv.* OFT; often 3, 6, 29; *ful oft*, repeatedly 24

on, *prep. w. dat.* ON 13, 66, 75; in 85, 109, 114 n.; *w. acc.* onto 32, 47, 52, 63, 74 (see **weg**); *adv.* 91 n.

oncweþan, *v. (5)*, answer, call in reply; **oncwæð** *p.t.* 23 n.

oncyrran, *w.v. (1)*, change (direction), turn aside, 103 *(reflex.)*.

ond, (MS 7), *conj.* AND 21, 29, 78, 85, etc.

ondrǣdan, *v. (7)*, DREAD, fear 106

ōnettan, *w. v. (1)*, hasten on, quickens 49

onhrēran, *w.v. (1)*, stir, move 96

onmēdla, *m. n-stem*, pomp, magnificence 81

onsȳn, *f. i-stem*, appearance; face 91

oþþe, *conj.* OR 70, 114

oðþringan, *v. (3)*, wrest (life from a person) 71

ōwiht, *n. i-stem*, AUGHT, anything 46

R

reord, *f. ō-stem*, voice 53

rīce, *n. ja-stem*, realm 81

S

sār, *n. a-stem*, [SORE]; pain 95

sāwol, *f. ō-stem*, SOUL 100

sǣ, *f. and m. i-stem*, SEA 14, 18

sǣfōr, *f. ō-stem*, SEA-voyage 42

sceal, see **sculan**

scēat, *m. a-stem*, [SHEET]

corner, region; *eorþan scea-tas*, the expanse of the earth 61 n., 105

sceolde, see **sculan**

sculan, *w.v. pret. pres.* [SHALL]; must, have to; **sceal,** *pres. 3. sg.* 109; **scyle,** *pres. subj. sg.* should 111; *on weg scyle*, must depart 74; **sceolde,** *p.t.* 30

scūr, *m. a-stem,* SHOWER; storm 17

scyle, see **sculan**

se (sē), sēo, þæt (i) *dem. adj. and def. art.* that, the; **se,** *m.* 12, 55, 94, 103, 106b; **þām,** *dat.* 122; **sēo,** *f.* 103, 107; **þā,** *acc.* 120; **þǣre,** *dat.* 100; **þæt,** *n.* 94, 108; **þā,** *pl.* 10, 56 (see **sum**), 57, 87; (ii) *dem. pron.*; **sē,** *m.* he 104; *se þe*, he who 27, 47, 106, 107; **þām,** *dat.* 51; **þæt,** *n.* that, it 12, 24, 55, 99, 109; *rel.* that 74; **þæs,** *gen.* for that 122 (see **þæs,** *adv.* 39, 40, 41); **þon,** *instr.* see **for; þā,** *pl.* those (things) 50

sealtȳþ, *f. jō-stem,* SALT sea-wave 35

sēarian, *w.v.* (*2*), [SEAR]; wither, fade 89

gesēcan, *w.v.* (*1*), SEEK, go to 38

secg, *m. ja-stem,* man 56

secgan, *w.v.* (*3*), SAY, relate 2

sefa, *m. n-stem,* mind, heart 51

***sēftēadig,** *adj.* blessed with comfort 56 n.

sēo, see **sē**

seofian, *w,v.* (*2*), lament, sigh 10

simle, *adv.* always 68

sind, *pres. 3 pl.* are 64, 80, 86; **sȳ,** *pres. subj.* (may there) be 122

singan, *v.* (*3*), SING, cry 22, 54

sīþ, *m. a-stem,* [SITHE]; journey, voyaging 51; experience 2

siþþan, *adv.* since; afterwards 78

slāt, see **slītan**

slītan, *v.* (*1*), [SLIT]; tear, rend; **slāt,** *p.t.sg.* 11

snīwan, *w.v.* (*1*), SNOW 31

song, *m. a-stem,* SONG 19

sorg, *f. ō-stem,* SORROW 54; anxiety 42

sōðgied, *n. ja-stem,* true lay, a lay about actual events (as distinct from many on legendary themes) 1

stānclif, *n. a-stem,* [STONE + CLIFF]; rocky cliff, crag 23

gestaþelian, *w.v.* (*2*), establish 104; make steadfast 108

staþol, *m. a-stem,* foundation; *healdan on staþelum,* keep in place, control 109

stearn, *m. a-stem,* [STERN, *sb.*[1]]; tern 23 n.

stefna, *m: n-stem,* STEM (of ship), prow 7

stīeran, *w.v.* (*1*) *w. dat.* STEER, control 109

stīþ, *adj.* firm 104

stondan, *v.* (*6*), STAND; remain, endure 67

storm, *m. a-stem,* STORM 23

strēam, *m. a-stem,* STREAM; *pl.* seas, ocean 34

strēgan, *w.v.* (*1*), STREW, spread 97 n.

strong, *adj.* STRONG, headstrong 109

sum, *pron.* SOME (one); one 68, *þa sume,* those (people) 56 n.

sumer, *m. a- u-stem,* SUMMER 54

swā, *adv.* SO, thus 51; *conj.* as 90

swēg, *m. i-stem,* sound, noise, music 21

swēte, *adj. as sb.* SWEET 95

geswincdagas, *m. pl.* DAYS of toil or hardship 2

swīþ, *adj.* mighty, strong 115

swylc, *rel. pron.* SUCH as 83

swylce, *adv.* likewise 53

sȳ, see **sind**

sylf, *adj.* SELF; *ic sylf,* I myself 35; *be me sylfum,* about myself 1

synn, *f. jō-stem,* SIN 100

T

tīd, *f. i-stem,* [TIDE]; time 124 (*acc.*)

tīddeg, *m. a-stem,* [TIDE + DAY]; span of life, final hour *69 n.

tilian, *w.v.* (*2*), [TILL, *v.*[1]]; labour (for), endeavour 119

tō, *prep. w. dat. or instr.* TO 43, 51, 61, 69; of, about (after noun of thinking) 44; in (marking the object in which delight is taken) 45; (of time) for 79 (see **ealdor**); (purpose) for, as 20, 101; *w. infin.* 37; *w. gen., to þæs,* to that degree, so 40, 41; *adv.* thereto 119 n.

tōgēanes, *prep. w. dat.* against 76

twēo, *m.* [TWO]; doubt, uncertainty 69

þ

þā, þām, see **se**

þās, see **þes**

þǣr, *adv.* THERE 18, 23a; *rel. conj.* where 6, 23b, 121; whereas 10

þǣre, see **se**

þǣs, *adv.* (*orig. gen.*) to that degree, so 39, 40; in *to þæs* see **tō**

þæt, *dem. adj., def. art. and pron.* see **se**

þæt, *conj.* THAT 34, 37, 42, 67, 123; (so) that 77, 119

þe, *indecl. rel. pron.* who, which 27, 47, 51, 57, 100, 106, 107; *þe him,* to whom 13; as *conj. particle* in *þeah þe* see **þeah**

þēah, *adv. and conj.* THOUGH; *þeah þe* 97, 113

þencan, *w.v.* (*1*), THINK 96; *swa þenceð,* is so minded 51

geþencan, *w.v.* (*1*), reflect, consider 118

þenden, *conj.* while 102

þēos, see **þes**

þes, *adj.* THIS; **þēos,** *f.* 86; **þās,** *acc. sg.* 87; **þis,** *n.* 65

þider, *adv.* THITHER 118

þing, *n. a-stem,* [THING]; condition, circumstance; *þinga gehwylce,* in all circumstances, without fail 68

þis, see **þes**

geþōht, *m. a-stem,* THOUGHT 34

þon, see **se** and **for**

þonc, *m. and n. a-stem* (*w. gen.*), THANKS 122

þonne, *adv.* then 118, 119; *conj.* when 8, 84, 102; *þonne . . . þonne,* then . . . when 94; than 65, 116

þrēo, *num.* THREE; *þreora sum,* one of three things 68

þringan, *v.* (*3*) [THRONG]; press; **geþrungen,** *p.pt.* constricted 8

þrōwian, *w.v.* (*2*), suffer 3

geþrungen, see **þringan**

þurh, *prep. w. acc.* THROUGH, by way of 88 n.

U

unþinged, *adj.* unprepared for, unexpected 106

unwearnum, *adv.* irresistibly 63

uprodor, *m. a-stem,* the heavens above 105

ūrigfeþra, *adj.* dewy-feathered 25

ūsic, see **wē**

uton, *pres. 1 pl. subj.* (*orig. of witan*), let us 117

W

wāc, *adj.* not firm, (morally) weak; *compar.* inferior, degenerate 87

wāt, see **witan**

wǣg, *m. i-stem,* wave 19

wǣron, *p.t.pl.* WERE 9, 83

wē, *pron. pl.* WE 117, 118, 119;
ūsic, *acc.* US 123

gewealc, *n. a-stem,* rolling,
tossing 6, 46

weard, *m. a-stem,* warder,
guardian 54

weg, *m. a-stem,* WAY; *on weg*
AWAY 74

weorþan, *v.* (*3*), [WORTH, *v.*[1]]
become; *to tweon weorþeð,*
proves a matter of un-
certainty 69

geweorþian, *w.v.* (*2*), hon-
our, exalt 123

wer, *m. a-stem,* man 21

wēr, *f.* covenant, pledge
110 n.

wērig, *adj.* WEARY, exhausted
29

wīde, *adv.* WIDELY, far and
wide; **wīdost,** *superl.* farthest, to very distant regions 57

wīf, *n. a-stem,* WIFE; woman
45

willan, *w.v. anom.* WILL; wish
(to) 97, 113; intend 43;
nille (*w. neg.*) will not
*99 n.

wine, *m. i-stem,* friend 115

winemǣg, *m. a-stem,* friend
and kinsman, dear kins-
man 16

wīngāl, *adj.* merry with wine
29

winter, *m. u-stem,* WINTER 15
(*acc.*)

gewis, *adj.* true, trustworthy
110 n.

wīse, *f. n-stem,* [WISE, *sb.*]
manner, way of living
110

witan, *w.v. pret. pres.* [WIT,
WOT]; know, realise; **wāt,**
pres. 3 sg. 12, 55, 92

gewītan, *v.* (*1*), go (away),
depart *52; **gewitene,**
p.pt. 80, 86

wið, *prep. w. acc. and dat.*
WITH; against 75, with
towards 112

wlitigian, *w.v.* (*2*), brighten,
make beautiful 49 n.

wlonc, *adj.* proud, splendid,
rich 29

wong, *m. a-stem,* meadow
49

geworht, see **gewyrcan**

woruld, *f. ō-stem,* WORLD 45,
49, 87

wrǣcca, *m. n-stem,* [WRETCH];
wanderer, exile 15

wrǣclāstas, *m.pl.* tracks o.
exile; *wrǣclastas lecgað,*
direct their exiled steps,
travel 57

wrecan, *v.* (*5*), [WREAK];
utter, recite 1

wuldor, *n. a-stem,* [WULDER];
glory 123

wunian, *w.v.* (*2*), dwell in,
remain on 15; live 87

wyn(n), *f. i-* or *jō-stem,* delight, pleasure 27, 45

gewyrcan, *w.v.* (*1*), WORK, accomplish, earn 74; *p.pt.* in *his geworhtne wine,* the friend he has made 115 n.

wyrd, *f. i-stem,* fate; (as the working of God's will) Doom 115 n.

Y

yldo, *f. īn-stem,* [ELD, *sb.²*]; age, old age 70, 91

ylfetu, *f.* (wild) swan 19 (*gen.*)

ymb, ymbe, *prep. w. acc.* around 11; about, of 46

ȳþ, *f. jō-stem,* wave 6, 46